CHOOSE

Your

UNIVERSE

CHOOSE *Your* UNIVERSE

AN EXERCISE IN FREEDOM

ATHENA IN TRUTH

CHANNELED BY ROBIN JELINEK

PUBLISHING

CHOOSE YOUR UNIVERSE

An Exercise in Freedom

ISBN		
	978-1-5445-3920-1	*Hardcover*
	978-1-5445-3919-5	*Paperback*
	978-1-5445-3918-8	*Ebook*
	978-1-5445-3921-8	*Audiobook*

I would like to dedicate this book to my mother,
who, by her actions, taught me how to give selflessly.

My mom was a woman of selfless action, not sappy words.
It wasn't until I got older and had my own family
that I realized this. She didn't know how to tell you she
loved you, but her actions always spoke of love.

I didn't get to tell her often enough how much
I appreciated her and how grateful I was for her example.
I know she will be smiling someplace when she sees this.

CONTENTS

FOREWORD

ROBIN AND I MET IN our early teens. Growing up in a small, upper-Midwest town, we had the same goals and aspirations, like building a home and starting a family and business. We continued to be best friends throughout our relationship and handled the challenges of marriage and running a business together.

Robin has always been there for anyone who needed help, and somehow those who needed help were always drawn to her. Maybe her passion for reading and learning about spirituality had something to do with it.

For forty-plus years, I have followed Robin in pursuit of her passion, and the information she shared resonated with me, so it must also resonate with others.

My life changed through a few sessions I had with a channeler—I was with Robin. The first session confirmed to me that what I was experiencing was real; the sessions that followed changed my life.

Many people who have had an experience with a channeler also want to become one. For over twenty years, Robin knew inside that she would become a channeler, but she never shared that knowing with anyone.

My son Mike and I were present when this powerful group of nonphysical beings burst through Robin on a full-moon evening, while overlooking the ocean. We were excitedly shocked but not surprised. Seven beings named themselves with distinct personalities that night, and five more showed up within the following year.

Wow! What a ride this has been! It has been like a whole new family!

(There is much more craziness leading up to and during the process of the group getting acclimated to Robin's body, which only channelers and their families understand.) This book was written for everyone who wants to improve their life and relationships by teaching them how to manifest exactly what they want. Readers will learn how to listen to themselves and choose what's best for them.

Choose Your Universe. Use the life gift you were born with: free will and choice.

— *Dave Jelinek*, Robin's husband

. . .

I hope the words in this book, channeled by Robin to convey Athena in Truth's words, will bring healing and peace to your life, as they have mine.

Robin is my sister and has always been someone who has lived her life in service to others. She is someone I treasure in life—I am grateful for our relationship and our common paths.

She is an authentic being that has endured the same struggles many of us have experienced. For a number of years, Robin and I and several other family members have been on a spiritual journey. We have read many books, tried various modalities, and delighted in the magic of learning of the existence of channelers and the knowledge and healing they have brought forth. We often joked about how fun it would be to have a channeler who we could ask questions of any time we wanted.

And then it happened—Robin became a channeler. In the beginning, Robin had very little time to talk to herself because several other family members and I constantly asked Athena in Truth questions.

Over the past eighteen years, I have done a good deal of work on myself, but the group's guidance has accelerated my growth—they have helped me understand that getting what you want doesn't come from condemnation but the *love* of self. This has freed me of my need to be perfect and given me the space to relax and enjoy living.

The information contained in this book is powerful yet very simple to apply. I think people tend to overcomplicate things, and Athena in Truth helps us see it can be *easy* to live our best lives. All we need to do is get out of our own way.

May this book show you that you are enough, even if you think you are not. You are a powerful creator who is a unique expression of the whole, and whatever you contribute, large or small, is expanding it.

Much love and gratitude.

— *Heidi Fralick*, Robin's sister

. . .

The first thing I noticed when I found out my mom could channel was the blunt and to-the-point communication. Anyone who knows my mom knows she's a very gentle and soft spoken person—the contrast between her natural state and the group's delivery is undeniable. Yet the depth and wisdom transmitted aligns with my mom's lifelong dedication to her spiritual growth. My mom has spent this life in service to others, enduring more than her share of suffering and embodying what it means to surrender. She now chooses how she wants to feel and surrenders to experiences—she no longer becomes them. I've often said to my wife that if I lived 1,000 lifetimes, I likely would not get another mother like this one. Her selflessness, infinite generosity, and compassion for others are what drew Athena in Truth to my mom.

This book comes at an amazing time—we can consume this type of information without the fear of physical harm or condemnation that has plagued other eras. I'm hopeful the words and techniques in this book will find the reader who needs them to grow and find more peace.

— *Brad Jelinek*, Robin's eldest son

. . .

As the youngest son, experiencing my mom as Athena in Truth has been very normal and comfortable. I was present the first day some of the group started speaking through her, and I felt an overwhelming sense of curiosity as I observed it. There wasn't any fear or confusion—simply a wanting to know more of what was happening. I even invited whoever was coming through her to come out because I just had a feeling something different was happening.

Since I experienced everything early on and have continued to be around my mom and the group, it's been impressive to see the development and transition from something that was raw into something that is now sharp. Athena in Truth is now part of the family, and for some reason, it is perfectly normal. There is no old Mom or new Mom—there's only an extra energy that appears from time to time. Sometimes Athena shows up when we are goofing around; other times we are arguing, and sometimes I am being soothed—it is similar to how I interact with my mom when she *isn't* channeling Athena. It's no different than a "normal" family dynamic—the group Athena speaks for is supportive, caring, and loving—except the communication is happening through my mom.

Sometimes it's hard to explain something knowingly strange to others that feels normal to you. All of my friends know my mom, love her, and recognize her kindness, generosity, and down-to-earth nature, but I think they might find it odd to know she is channeling Athena in Truth. Anyone who *truly* knows my mom would never question her genuine nature or authenticity, and I can tell you that if anything here was inauthentic or fake, our family (my brother and I included) would be the first to call bullshit!

Being able to engage with Athena and the group has been a great learning experience for me. Overall, the best lesson I've learned and developed is the ability to listen to and trust my intuition. It's never been stronger, and now when I know I feel something, I know *why* or that I need to explore it.

—*Mike Jelinek*, Robin's youngest son

WHO IS ATHENA?

ATHENA IN TRUTH is a collective of non-physical entities channeled by Robin Jelinek. The group is represented by one of the entities, Athena, who transmits consciousness for the entire group. Throughout this book, Athena will be referred to as "we" and "they" as a reminder that they are not a single cognition.

The group's stated purpose is to help people become aware that they have the ability to create their lives in any way they choose. Athena helps people get on the right track and live the life they came here to live by showing us how to use our own internal guidance system to grow into our power.

Athena in Truth exists at a higher level of consciousness.

You have a higher level of consciousness too. Whether you are focused here on earth or any other existence, that higher aspect of you still exists at the same time. The consciousnesses of Athena in Truth are merged together to provide you a higher perspective on what you are, who you are, and who you came to be.

Once you gain that understanding, then you will understand who *we* are. We are the source, an emanation of all that is—you are *also* the source, an emanation of all that is. Part of you expresses itself in human form, while the source part of you guides you on your journey through the use of emotional communication.

Through our connection to Robin, we communicate using her body, or her vessel. You are using *your* vessel to communicate for *you*, so in essence we are the same.

A NOTE FROM ROBIN

AS I, ROBIN, TYPE THIS TEXT, I do it with no idea what I will write. This requires a great deal of trust and allowing that can, at times, be challenging. The best way I can describe it to you is to imagine you were out to dinner, and the couple talking behind you mentioned your name. Your interest would be piqued, but you wouldn't want to be rude to the person you were with by focusing your attention on the couple's conversation. This is similar to what can sometimes happen to me when channeling. My consciousness becomes piqued, and I quickly have to control that awareness so I stay in the flow.

They don't speak to me and tell me what to write—there is no direct communication. It just flows through my fingers, and as it does, I watch the words appear on the screen. When I explain to others (like you) how natural this feels for me, I also explain that all humans are already doing this, though they may have more brain coherence than I do.

You don't have to know everything that is coming, and you

don't have to plan out every detail. You can simply allow your desires to unfold through you by choosing to be happy.

Throughout this book, you will gain the understanding that you have free will, meaning the ability to choose. No longer will you be a victim of your circumstances and be trapped within your negative emotions. You will learn how to become a master to your human partner by allowing your source to govern you. All of the tools that you will need to achieve the life that you came here to live will be revealed to you.

When I decide to write, I relax and allow the higher consciousness of the group to transmit the text right through my hands. I know that it will come—I never doubt or worry about it. I am forever surprised by how easy transmitting is. Through this experience, I have come to understand how being in the flow feels and how easy it is supposed to be. When you decide how something will be and you allow it to be, it is effortless.

I originally thought about writing a book years ago, and I now realize that this was a part of my blueprint or life plan. When I tried to write back then, however, I found it very difficult. Finally, I decided, *This is not for me. I am not a writer.*

I remember many years ago, Dave and I were headed out of town, and we stopped at a bookstore to pick up a coffee on our way. While I was waiting for my coffee, a small book on the shelf caught my attention. I picked it up and within the first few pages read, "What if you are just projecting yourself into your body?"

It was as though a light went on in that moment that I was never able to turn off. I remember telling Dave, word for word, what I had read and how much it resonated with me. We spent the rest of the drive talking about this possibility.

What if we are just projecting ourselves into the bodies we have? Could this be possible?

I spent many years studying literally hundreds of books on every spiritual topic that I could find, gaining a great deal of knowledge. I didn't know at the time that this knowledge would benefit me in my future doing the work that I now do.

It is important that you understand I am not a writer—I am a channeler for a writer. Athena, a higher consciousness, dictates the text. Starting with the Introduction, everything that follows was dictated by Athena. I allowed Athena to take over as the writer in order to accomplish what we needed to accomplish.

How is it that I can write so easily now? I believe it can be done and trust completely in the process, so I receive it effortlessly.

You, *too*, can forget yourself and allow the high part of you to transmit through you. When you can forget yourself and trust, you can align to a higher form of consciousness that allows you to connect to abilities you otherwise would not be aware of.

I know it seems a bit easier for me in my case because of my unique circumstances, but I promise that you also have the power to do great things—if you so choose. If it were your desire to become a channeler, you could become one. Through that desire, you would be drawn to do the things that support that endeavor. As you read this book, you will learn how to receive and achieve anything you want on this earth.

You have to ask, believe, and allow; then you can receive. It is really that simple.

Introduction

YOU ARE
ALL CHANNELERS

⎯⎯⎯⎯⎯⎯⟶

YOU ARE THE BEST EXAMPLE of a channeler. You would not be in the body you are in if you were not channeling through it.

Every experience you've ever had, and all you have grown in your individualistic form, still exists all the time. It is never over or gone—it keeps becoming more. *You are source energy* that is experiencing you as you. *You* are expanding with every experience you have. There is no judgment, no right or wrong. Only expansion.

What you do or do not do doesn't matter—you become more *because* of all your experiences. The goal here is to attain mastery and recognize your free will and ability to choose how you respond to your experiences. It is more about gaining the awareness that you have come here to embody your source, and as such, you will see in form how great you have become by what you have experienced.

It is important that you realize how natural your connection is and that you believe and trust in it. There is *never* a time when your high self will not respond to you. There is never a time that someone *else's* high self will not respond to you. All you need to do is ask and then *trust* in the communication you receive.

Asking and trusting is going to feel natural because it's *you*. Some of you think connecting with your higher self will produce a big moment or something otherworldly. All that occurs is your belief and ability to perceive yourself as the source. The source is love. It is the energy of positivity. The source that you emanate from, that is really all that exists, is ever-expanding love. When you emanate from the source and take physical form, it becomes harder to keep that connection and understanding while also allowing yourself to submerge in the environment you've chosen to experience. As you add more contrast, or become separated from your source, it becomes harder to remember who you are because you are projecting a version of yourself into everything you are experiencing. As a result, your objective is to remember what you are and what you have access to.

Some of you will channel in spoken words or through writing, such as I do. Some of you will channel with music, art, or your profession.

Your comparison or judgment about what someone else does is inhibiting you from doing what *you* are capable of doing.

All of it is divine, and when you apply your divinity in any way, it is worthy. Do not discount any of it. The expression you are using is unique to you, so honor it, believe it, and *know* it.

As you learn to trust, you will fling the doors open like an excited child on the last day of school. There is nothing that will be denied to you except what you deny yourself. You do not need to be a perfect human in order to receive what you are desiring—you are a human who is governed by source. *All* of you are.

When you have an interest or desire, whether it be in work, spirituality, or whatever you are called to, *that* is your divine nature. The passion is the source. Quit trying to define it in a way that is like someone else. If you have a calling, desire, or strong passion, *that* is your source. When you have a path (and you are naturally drawn to it), you can't get enough of it, or you are driven in some way to anything, that drive is coming from your source. It's your higher self trying to lead you down the road of life that you already created *prior* to coming to earth. You are given this passion so you can remember what you wanted to create and, most importantly, how you wanted to feel. It's an assistive quality to help you achieve your desired purpose.

Expression in Form Is Source in Form

Are you having an "aha" moment?

Are you realizing you are it and whatever calls you is it?

Maybe you never realized that expression in form is *source* in form. I am talking about music, singing, art—all of it. When you are in a connected state, you are in alignment with all that is. You are channeling. It is an expression from your higher self through you. There simply is no creation without the creator, so stop thinking source has to be something other than what you already are.

A desire is your source calling you to what you wish to express, and if you follow that desire, it will not disappoint you.

How is it that you want what you want? This is your source supplying you with emotions based upon the thoughts it is receiving from you. Thoughts of negativity mean you're moving away from your joy, alignment, and the life you intended. Positivity means you are moving toward it.

When I was in my mid twenties, I could feel a desire to understand more about who I was and what I was doing here. All of these questions created a quest to absorb as much information as I could about spirituality and how it applied to life. Along the way I met a channeler, which gave me exposure to the situation I now find myself in. None of this was random.

You don't get on a bus, an airplane, or a cab where the other people are not energetically matched to you. They may be your match in something you like or something you don't like, but make no mistake—these people are not there by mistake. Everything in your life is being created. Every single place you go, every breath you take, and everything you do, *you* are the creator of.

So you see, *you* are the creator, and *you* are working in union with all that is. You experience; you generate feelings and desires, and the universe responds with passion, so you achieve those objectives.

You are everything who can be anything; all you need to do is choose it.

Humans Are Unhappy

Too many humans are unhappy. Many people want to blame their circumstances, situations, current events—*anything* but themselves. But *you* are the chooser. *You* are the creator of everything you have in your life. If you are unhappy, it's because *you* have chosen it.

You just don't know it.

You think things are done *to* you. You have bad luck, or you're a victim of your circumstances. It is my hope that by the time you are finished reading this book, you will stop blaming everyone and everything else for your unhappiness and choose to be happy instead.

As long as you continue to blame external factors, you are not going to change. You are going to continue to be unhappy. You won't get the life you wanted to get because you are not aware that what you are doing is having an impact upon your life.

When you start to blame your environment, your bank account, or other people instead of realizing you are the chooser of everything around you, you will be unhappy. You have the choice to move on from anything that brings you unhappiness.

You can decide to look at everything in your life as a detriment. Your husband, your children, your job—you can look at what you don't want or like about each thing, or you can use your focus and decide that life is a *lovely* thing. Once you choose to focus on life as a good thing, all the things in your life you *don't* like will gently fall away. It's why you have it, why you are having the experience that you are. Focus is your creative power as a human.

For example, if you focus on how much your mate is not a match to you, you will regenerate the very thing you do not prefer. The whole reason for the experience is for you to decide on a preference. Once that is accomplished, put all of your energy into that, and let the universe bring you your preference. Know that whenever you have a preference, it will be reflected in your interactions, both positive and negative.

Sometimes you choose to make your decisions based only upon your human and its present emotional state. When you become unified with your source, you will feel the emotions, but you will not be overtaken by them. You will understand that you have free will, and when used correctly, it is about making choices from a place that makes you feel the best in any given situation. In this way your human will rise and align with your source, and the universe delivers to those who align. This is how you get the life you were meant to have.

You can attract in misery or happiness. If you attract in misery, you're simply going to attract more of what is making you miserable. When you focus on what you don't like, you will end up in another situation that is just as bad because of the backward way you focused. One bad situation will end, and another will begin.

Focus on what you like:

- This is what I would love a mate to be like.

- This is how I want to feel.

- These are the people I love to work with.

Instead of:

- I don't want to see that jerk behind the desk.

- I want out of here.

- I don't like my husband; he's lazy.

You may get rid of him by focusing on what you don't like, but you're going to attract another just like him.

Many people ask, "If I'm going to be happy, how do I get out of these situations I don't like?"

Focusing on what you *do* like is the only way out. You don't get away from an unhappy situation by being unhappy about it, blaming and pointing fingers, and deciding it is awful. That may clear you of the things you don't like, but when you are focused on what makes you unhappy, you attract the same quality back to you again. Instead, put your focus on what you do want and what makes you happy. By doing this, anything that is not a match to that focus will disappear from your experience.

Your Problem

You're reading this book either because you don't have the life you expected or because you have what you wanted but are still not happy. You're looking for something outside of yourself to feel better.

You may have picked up this book to get higher wisdom. Understand that any higher wisdom will be coming from you. You may feel you are a victim and would like someone else to fix you, but you must do this for yourself. You are not powerless. You are powerful. This book will offer you a reminder of how to embrace your power.

What You'll Get from This Book

By reading this book, you are going to realize you are 100 percent responsible for the life you have. You will understand that every day you create an environment, a *life*, for yourself.

How do you want it to be?

Will you continue to focus on everything you don't like, not realizing you are re-creating more of what you *don't* like?

Or will you learn to use your focus by directing it and manifesting all the things you *do* want?

You are the creator of the life unfolding before you because you have free will. Throughout this book, you are going to learn how to think in a way that will help you achieve the life you want.

The point of this book is not to teach you to channel (though I won't discount that it could be the key to unlock *your* door), but it will teach you how to manifest. This book will teach you how to ask for anything you want and anything you want to be, including a channeler, by following the clues from your higher self through your guidance system.

While you read this book, use your guidance system. Your guidance system is the feeling you get in response to every emotion. It's the feeling you get in response to a person you've just met or a situation you are in. This feeling is you being guided by your higher self. Your guidance system is always between you and you. How you are thinking is bringing you closer to your source or moving you further from it. It's your job to listen to this guidance system. Let's say there is someone you can't stand. You justify it by the things they do (or are) that you judge as reasons for not liking them. You feel negative emotions, not because any of this is necessarily true but because the universe is receiving you in that negativity and producing on that negative focus.

How will it respond? More people who you don't like or possibly other situations that will evoke similar negative emotions.

Either way you're being notified, so pay attention and adjust accordingly to feel in a way that will benefit you.

You will say, "How can I? They irritate me."

We will reply, "Be grateful for them showing you that there is active irritation energy within you. They would never have shown up in your experience if you were not somehow a match to them."

To be clear, the guidance system is responding to you only. It isn't about a right or wrong path; there isn't one. It's about how you think in regard *to* the path. You cannot achieve anything that you are not undividedly behind. Clarity is focus, without contradiction. When you focus on something and have apprehension, that is what the guidance system will respond to, not that what you are focused on is wrong. Remember there is no good or bad; there is only focus. Your guidance system will respond to that.

Think about how you want to feel. Decide whether you agree with what you're reading, and then go with that feeling. Mark the important places you feel pertain to you. Reference yourself back to them, and be conscious of how you create what you focus on.

When you ask for something and you expect to get it—when you understand the principle *of* getting it—you *are* going to get it.

Once you finish reading this book, ask to be guided to live the life you came here to live:

"I really want to achieve the life I came here to achieve. From now on, I will only draw things to myself that will benefit me. Now that I have asked, I know that I have received what I am asking for. It will infiltrate my entire being the moment I have asked."

This is the most important step. Once you have completed asking, move into belief. There will be nothing you need to do or force. Now you are in receiving mode.

You'll turn around and think, *How did that happen? How did I completely transform myself in areas where I was stuck for years?* Because you could never do it by yourself. You had to ask the source within you. You, the human, is the vessel, but the source is the transformation of you.

Why We Are Here

I believe the group consciousness called Athena in Truth has come to assist in the rising of consciousness. The teaching of choosing your expression, rather than reacting to it, is the key that elevates thinking and gives way to new thoughts and higher consciousness.

For quite some time, there has been opposition energy in many areas of the world. Everyone is beginning to choose sovereignty and that choosing has created a tipping point.

More and more people are realizing they are the creator. They understand that they know how they feel, what to do, and how to get where they want to be. As they begin to understand how they create, there will be no need for jealousy or any concern about what others have because everyone will understand how to get what they want in their lives.

For instance, COVID-19 enabled many people to get out of the job they were stuck in, and they started to realize they could do something they enjoyed instead. This raised the vibratory level of the entire planet.

You have the ability to perceive the world in your sovereignty. You are not a victim—you are a creator based upon your focus and ability to direct it.

There have been many teachings that have veered off from what is truth. We have forgotten our ability as determiners of truth and have begun to be followers of the masses. Masses can have a mob mentality. Once someone starts to run, everyone else runs, yet they have no idea why they are running. Be very mindful of why you are running and what—or who—you are choosing to follow.

Don't get caught up in the masses' beliefs of right and wrong because they don't exist. Someone has focused, chosen, and decided to believe, and now others are following blindly. Be your own chooser, follower, focuser, and *decider* of all that you perceive. That's all you have; it's the whole basis of the life you will create. Do it uniquely, individually, and sovereignly. This is the expression of you.

Each of you is experiencing life based upon your own views of it. There will never be two of you who are alike. There will never be two who do it the same, nor should there be. In order for the universe to expand and grow, this is necessary. No one should pretend to be something they're not in order to copy another or decide the person they are isn't good enough or should contribute more.

If you look at every person on earth—their lives, how they perceive themselves, and how others perceive them—you're never going to find a duplicate. The universe is expanding because of this growth. If everyone tried to be the same, there would be no expansion *or* growth.

Everything you add to the universe by the experiences you have is fresh, innovative, new, and expansive. None are better than, higher than, or more *valuable* than any others.

Reconnect with Your Higher Self

I get many questions about what I do in channeling sessions. Even though there are words exchanged, what really occurs is an *energy* exchange. When someone engages openly in a session, they are brought to a resonance equal to their higher self.

When I do a session with someone, Athena temporarily merges with the client's higher self, and the client always recognizes it. Everyone has an energetic code their higher self connects to in order to receive the experiences they are having. When Athena connects with their higher self, they connect through this code, and the client can feel their higher self through a kick to their guidance center. It's similar to putting your palm upon a door that is electronically charged to know you.

This resonance opens them up to surpass the self-perceptions that have been holding them back because they're temporarily lifted to a higher vibratory level, which transcends the perceptions and false beliefs that a human holds upon the earth. They are returned to their magnificence, hope, understanding, wisdom, and knowing of the power they are.

How you open yourself to your higher self is different for everyone. How you open up depends on your journey and your genetic code. There are many practices a human can follow: silent retreat, meditation, chakra balancing, breathwork. For some, these practices may do nothing at all to unlock their doors. They may fall on their tailbone, set off their Kundalini,[1] and have a full-blown awakening. There is only one way: your way.

I did many spiritual practices, and one of them was chakra balancing (more on this topic in Chapter 1), which was the key that unlocked my door. But that door was already going to be unlocked through my desire to know more, do more, be more, reach my potential, and connect to my passion. As you depart on your own journey toward what you desire in your life, you will be guided. Then, when you have an interest in something, recognize it as a sign from all that is. Continue following these breadcrumbs until you find what you are searching for.

When someone becomes *obsessed* with having this knowledge and wisdom (like I was), when they can't get enough of it and *never* stop reading and researching, they will have their awakening *or* the opportunity to know and expand *more*. This desire to learn and expand is what will unlock their doors.

To accomplish what you want to accomplish, there has to be a passion that ignites you. People on a spiritual journey have the desire for an awakening. They may tell you they were doing breathwork, meditation, or something spiritual, and that is what they think unlocked their door, but it was the simple desire of *wanting* it to happen. That desire is why they are able to manifest.

The group's goal is to connect as many people as possible to the higher part of themselves in order for a shift to occur in the planet's energetic resonance. In the past, as many read

---

1   Kundalini is the life force energy that lives at the base of your spine in your root chakra and is often referred to as a coiled snake. When you have a Kundalini Awakening, this energy travels upward through each of your chakras and into your crown chakra and triggers a higher consciousness.

information and sought evolution through change, they lodged themselves into experiences, without the ability to move beyond them. They wouldn't realize they were stuck in their human and would shame themselves if they behaved in ways they did not deem as "right" or "spiritual." This often happens with people who embark on their spiritual path, but it's counterproductive to their growth and expansion. They begin to build a character, as they believe they have to act in a certain way: do this; don't do that. Before they know it, they condemn themselves, which won't get them anywhere.

In essence, they tried to change themselves, and this is impossible as a human. A human is a tool used to implement the higher self's influence. Without the influence of the high self, the human will be forever lodged in its experiences. When you're lodged in these experiences, judging yourself for not being spiritual enough or good enough, you can't move out of them. You keep regenerating the behavior that you're unhappy with. Many say, "I want to change. I don't want to behave like this." But they stay in that energy and continue to regenerate that weakness within themselves. They don't realize the only way they can change is by recognizing the higher self is the one who does the changing, and the human merely follows through in its actions.

Once the high self is recognized, reunited, and merged, everything wanted will automatically flow. When you welcome the guidance of your higher self through your emotional guidance system, you will be reunited in your power and in your understanding of where the power is coming from.

The group often tells clients, "Once you merge with your higher consciousness, there is no work to do. This is an automatic flow, a connection that has the ability to transform not only you, but the world." The way to get the most out of yourself and the source is to simply love yourself for experiencing. You came here to have life experiences and expand the whole through them. That is all you agreed to when you came here. Once you can perceive yourself in this way, there is no reason to ever condemn yourself.

If something happens that you're not liking, simply say to your higher self, "I would like to be better at this. I would like some assistance." Then, go about your merry way, feeling good again, and align to this energy of love and positivity. You, as a human, are not capable of delivering to yourself what you want. You simply need to ask the spirit to do it for you.

Isn't it wonderful to know there is no work to be done, other than to love yourself for the experiences you are contributing? That being a contributor is what you came to earth to do?

No one is judging you for how you contribute, except you. Be grateful for all you have and experience. Love yourself for the journey, and use your physical form to emanate your source to all you come into contact with.

Fear, separation, and judgment are *all* a part of the false belief you have somehow unperformed to an arbitrary level of perfection.

Many of us believe we have to work hard to get the prize, and we believe it of our spirituality too:

"I must deny myself things I enjoy. I will not drink a glass of wine. I will eat only vegetables. I will force myself to meditate all day every day. There! Now I feel worthy of having because I have suffered enough to have it."

But it is not the suffering that has caused the manifestation; it is the *desire* you have and the way you justified it, perceived it, and then allowed it to be.

You don't have to work hard. You don't have to be miserable in order to be worthy to gain what you want. When you make yourself miserable, you give in to your perception that you are now worthy of having that which you are asking for, which is why you receive it. You believe you must contribute something to be worthy instead of just deciding: *I am worthy*.

You don't have to do anything to be worthy. You already are, no conditions attached.

Chapter 1

ARE THERE
TWO OF YOU?

WE ARE VERY GRATEFUL to have this opportunity to assist you in your life. We hope that as you read the words we transmit, you feel good. We want you to know we are doing nothing more than connecting you to *truth*, which is the primary reason you feel good as you read.

The truth is, there is one of you split into two: you the human (a.k.a. your tool or vessel) and your source (a.k.a. your soul or spirit). There is a dialog going on between you and your source—the human in its experiential form is communicating openly with your source in its emotional form. You are working together, one doing (the human) and one feeling (the source). Your human tool is acting as an experiencer of life, and the source receives that content and responds through emotions. Many of you think the *human* is generating the emotions, when in actuality your higher self is guiding you by sending emotional responses to your perceptions of your experiences. The human receives those responses and then chooses whether it will follow the guidance or remain in the emotion of their perception. You either become the human and are lodged in the experience, which creates suffering, or you choose to move from it in your higher perspective and live a life of joy.

The human is a feeling form: it experiences pain and pleasure and has needs. The source funds the human. It guides the human by making it feel good when it's headed in a direction that it perceives will be to its liking and making it feel terrible when it heads in a direction it perceives it won't like.

The human experiences and feels through all its senses. Then it decides by what it has felt whether it will embody the human in the experience it felt *or* whether it will embody its source in the remembrance of who it is, what it is, and why it came. As you embody your source, you choose. You choose in your free will, knowing that there is a lesson that leads to betterment.

This is the master, the one who remembers who they are, what they are, and why they have come. They don't become the emotions the human is feeling; they simply decide that they are the operator of the game piece, and they are going to use it in a way that they will win. They win through alignment, which is the understanding that all energy is being transmuted to the highest level of love, and they decide that they as a human tool have this ability. They as a human can see every experience and something they have to gain, and in this way, they become the winner.

Therein lies the greatest challenge for a human: they constantly think that those involved in their experiences are the problem or the things that justify their negativity. "They were rude. They were mean. They hurt me." All the while, they are the ones who have called to themselves every single experience they are having. So to figure out your communication between you and you—meaning you and your source—you have to know that that is what it is. All emotion is for you, about you, and about the way you are choosing to perceive. In order to get desired results in your life, you must perceive what there is in every exchange you have. "How am I thinking about this situation, and how am I feeling as I am doing it? If I am not feeling good, I am choosing to miss my teaching and to blame the one in front of me."

The human part of you has free will, and the source does not tell it what to eat, wear, or do. The source simply responds to what the human has chosen to do through emotional indicators, which are based upon both your life plan and the free will choice you have made in past lives and are making in this life.

We don't want to disappoint you when it comes to your human tool, but most of you give it more credit than it deserves. It is a wonderful tool for feeling, experiencing, and expanding, to be sure, but the value you put in the human is far greater than what it should be, especially in comparison to the part of you most humans don't have an understanding of: the source.

Now we realize that humans are on the physical plane, and there are mouths to feed, shelters to buy, and things you must do to survive. However, while you are doing that, it doesn't mean you can't desire something beyond it or create something else. You absolutely can, but you cannot do it from a place of hatred or dislike of where you are. If you do, you become stuck because the source is perceiving you exactly as you are feeling. It doesn't matter who you think has caused it. It is one thing, and that one thing is you. It is *your* emanation it receives, so the idea of justification becomes self-defeating; it can never serve you. You feel; you get.

Your source wants to remind your human to think positively, but your human gets confused by emotional responses from your source. How you feel carries a resonance, a signal, a rate of vibration, which has an attractive quality to it. Your preferences, based on those feelings, help you choose what you want more of or less of. The emotional charges coming from your source are there to guide you to move closer to or further from how you are perceiving.

All emotions carry a charge and creative value. Having any emotion, whether you deem it negative or positive, has creative potential, *provided* you don't attach to it. Why do you send the same signal by continuing to be justified in your emotions? Know that you have, in all that is, become the highest potential of the energy you release. There is never a need to keep sending the same signal. The desire to do that comes from the need to be right or justified in your belief that someone else is responsible for how you feel. The universe feels how you feel about everything, and it returns on that feeling. So if you are justifying a negative feeling, it's futile. You will only receive back the negativity you are justifying.

As you learn to feel and release, *everything* you feel can benefit you, as long as you don't *become* the negative experience and *hold* onto it.

In order to be able to create, your source must have freedom, which means you have to have total accountability and responsibility. Because as soon as you take that responsibility, you take power over that situation and release yourself from hatred and dislike. This means you benefit from your experiences and do not become victimized by them. You choose to grow from them and stop blaming the messengers for mirroring back to you what is within you. You are no longer giving any cognitive energy to it. In your recognition of this creation, you're choosing to align to it and will now receive it in form.

Self-love means loving yourself for having experiences. You are *not* a human—you are a god in human form. From this perspective you can choose to *learn* from your human experiences and instead attach to your source. This deliberate intent is your key to yourself.

You Are Limitless

You are an experiencer, an expansion seeker, and the source some call god. What you have viewed in your upbringing, your lineage, and the environment you have encompassed can limit you if you choose to become your experiences instead of picking and choosing how you will feel about them, but there is nothing higher than, better than, or more worthy than *you*. Once you can adopt this understanding, you can put away your fears, doubts, worries, and false beliefs of the limitations you have placed upon yourself.

One of the reasons you have both a lineage and present-day experiences is so that you can choose to expand yourself as your source perceives rather than how your human or past humans have perceived. You can actively choose to overcome past and present experiences and become the higher aspects of them and pass on a new legacy that your future lineage can take with them.

Many humans have viewed defeat, people who have failed,

and they have decided to agree with what they see. This limits them in what they are.

There is nothing a human cannot call to themselves, except for what they *decide* they can hold, perceive, or believe based upon what they have had exposure to. It takes a great amount of study and will to open oneself up to the new ideas we are presenting in this book, but you are limitless in what you can learn and what you can obtain in your life.

When we say you are limitless, we want you to think about how many ways belief-based expansion has happened to you. You may not have noticed at the time; you may not have *realized* you agreed with the things you were seeing, and yet, looking back, you understand you *did* and that belief is what caused the expansion. Put another way: your beliefs are causing manifestation in your life, both knowingly and unknowingly.

This is what we mean when we say you are an experiencer. You have come here as a human to experience and then draw *from* those experiences to develop your own set of perceptions and beliefs so you can create upon the earth.

The Freedom to Create

In order to create, you must have freedom, meaning total accountability and responsibility. As soon as you take that responsibility, you take power over that situation, which allows you to choose how you will feel based upon the lesson you have gotten from it. When you choose the alignment or navigate through the experience until you feel good, you will align to your creator and to what you have created through that experience.

But many of you have decided to follow what the masses believe and have given up your sovereignty (a.k.a. control over your life) to become robots. You have become believers of believers and fearful that something outside yourself has power over you. Let us reassure you: you are the power of you. Too many of you decide to give your power away in your agreement to what others fear. Don't do it. Live the beautiful, peaceful, wonderful lives that you can create for yourselves. When you look into the mirror and love what you see and feel, you are seeing yourself as your source sees you.

So many of you give up your choices, go along with the masses, and wonder why you don't feel good and don't have the life you had hoped for. You have been trained to please others and use their reflection of you as your truth.

This is mostly fear-based. Take down the walls you have placed around yourself by inadvertently thinking your emotions are your truth. Emotions do nothing more than reveal a choice, which produces your authentic truth.

Everyone is experiencing, perceiving, and forming beliefs based on those experiences and perceptions. The source flows through all things, but it can only flow to the degree *you* allow it to. It has to recognize itself as itself, which it does by being the same. You have to emanate back the match to what your source's emanation is: love.

When you become the human, you become the density of your reality, and your source can't flow through or reach you. This is separation and reveals itself in negativity.

Now you understand why you are negative—you have separated yourself from your positive source. You're consumed by your experience and have become it. You have come to earth to express you are a god in human form, not to *become* the human form.

The positive source is you and all that is. You are funding your tool, your human. When you separate yourself in your negativity, condemnation, shamefulness, and judgment, you lower your vibratory level to a degree that your higher self can no longer connect to. Now you are on the human plane in a lower level of consciousness, which is dense and where negativity is plentiful. The only way you can rise out of this negative space is to have a connection with the high part of yourself, which vibrates with the high energy of love. Sometimes you may feel like you can't connect or that you are lost in your experiences. When this happens, don't forget to call out to your source and ask it to join you. This is an option that many of you forget. In your recognition of who you are, what you are, and why you are here, there is alignment, and help is always available if you can't find that alignment. You simply have to ask.

When you find yourself surrounded by negativity, at first you may notice it and think that you need to avoid it so that you don't get sucked into it. But as you grow in your understanding, you will learn that there is nothing to avoid when you are not creating something negative. In other words, the negativity wouldn't be there unless you were already a match to it. Look inside yourself with love and compassion and say, "I love my human for letting me know I have somehow attracted something to myself that I do not want. Now I can move away from it, not in condemnation but in the recognition I have received the message I needed to get."

Look at what you are attracting to yourself, and examine why. If you look at your life and honestly notice what you have agreed to in mass consciousness, you will begin to see how it has infected your perception of the world. What you believe and have consciously agreed to is what the universe personally responds to.

Do you wish for the universe to respond to someone else's perceptions?

Or would you prefer the universe to respond to your own?

Start noticing, start questioning, and start creating the universe you personally choose.

You Are Your Own Universe

To help you understand there are two of you, think about it like this: almost everyone talks to themselves. Whether we scold ourselves during a bad shot at golf or tennis, or when we push ourselves to get a project done, we all can think of an incident where we've talked to ourselves.

If we notice, it is positive reinforcement of what we want—it is the human doing something the higher self wants.

However, some people scold themselves very harshly. That is not your higher self—it is your human judgment or perception of yourself. Encouragement, understanding, and belief are from the source part of you. We can respond in the human, or we can respond as the source.

You are a universe all of your own and a contributor to all that is. Your universe is responding to and interacting with all that is. You are a part of an attraction-based, intricate system responding to you in every "now" moment you are in. The universe is responding and interacting with all that is based upon what you perceive in your masses, as well as exclusively with you in your sovereignty. Where your focus is will determine what you have access to. If you focus individually for you and do not look out into the masses, then you are creating your personal universe. If you are constantly looking outside of yourself and adding the masses' opinions, ideas, and beliefs to your universe, you allow the masses to create within your experience.

What You Attract Is Attracting You

When a human finds themselves experiencing something not to their liking, they revert back to victimization and justification. They do not want to accept how they have attracted this unlikable thing.

To be fair, the detailed way the universe links people, situations, and circumstances to each other can vary greatly, but what *never* varies is the link to how you *feel*.

Say you experience a theft. There are a variety of ways you could experience theft that could attract it to you:

- You could be in lack.

- You could believe you're too smart to be tricked.

- You could despise thieves.

- You could worry about protecting yourself.

All of these feelings will result in attracting a thief to you.

We would advise you if you do experience something that you unknowingly attracted to yourself, try not to move to blame, anger, and despair because these emotions, when untethered, will also attract responses that you are not going to like.

Why do you humans have such a hard time with acceptance? Because when you are in your physical form, you are faced with all of your senses—what you're seeing and feeling. There are so many inputs overwhelming you in this form, it can be hard to separate yourself from what you have deemed to be your reality.

It is difficult to let go of either and perceive differently. This is why many humans choose victimization or blaming: because the senses make it very difficult to accept responsibility. They become the emotions *of* the human instead of responding to the source and knowing it sent the emotions because of separation.

When you see something in a form you don't prefer, it is difficult to let go of it and perceive differently. When a human becomes its experiences, though, it blames the experience or those that are a part of it *instead* of recognizing it is choosing to view it in a way that separates it from the higher self.

It's easy to get caught up in your emotions and the manifestation of whatever has occurred that is unfavorable. Unconsciously, you decide it's easier to believe life is random and that you're a victim rather than the idea that you've played a part in manifesting it. When something enters your universe and takes form, know you've somehow created it.

We like to tell humans to drop the bags. Don't deny the negative experience, condemn it, or blame yourself for it—drop the experience and decide to start creating what you really want. Accept what the experience is teaching. Know you're the creator of it. Be accountable, and consciously move yourself where you prefer. Don't wallow in the negative experience or try to justify it. Understand there are only creators who create and match one another.

Assert Your Sovereignty

We've told you many times to be more concerned with the perception of yourself rather than the perception others offer you.

Why would you decide to take someone else's perception?

Because they reflect back to you the false belief you hold for yourself.

You are pure, positive source energy. The part of you that never dies, that is joined to your higher self, comes from the high vibratory level of *love*. When you become unconscious of this truth, you have the possibility of losing your vibratory level.

When you come to the earth as a child, you come in your sovereignty, meaning you come with the understanding that you are god. There's nothing outside of you that's higher, better, bigger, or more powerful than you.

Every single person, over the course of their lives, has adopted a false belief that others are more powerful and more capable. This is nothing more than a lie they have chosen to believe. So when we tell you that you are the source, you can't accept it. Why can't you accept it? Because you have to find something in your human form that confirms the idea that you must be perfect in order to be worthy of your source. This is a false belief. Imagine your power and own it. It's yours. You are worthy just as you are.

Can you picture accepting it?

You are not your life experiences, or for a better term, the *result* of your life experiences. You are *consciousness* expressing itself and *experiencing* that expression.

Now more than ever, you are being challenged to assert your sovereignty. There is nothing more powerful than choosing the environment you want to see and not succumbing to the one being presented to you by the masses.

This change has been in the making for a long time—there has been a purging of materialism and a recognition of love and authenticity. There has been a dismantling of leadership and a cry for reverence—everything is being rearranged and taken apart.

How can you expect this to be a smooth transition? You are the ones in the midst of this great time of change.

We have reached the tipping point where going back is no longer an option—trying will be intolerable. As you expand to new conscious awareness and accept that you are the source, you are *love*, you will become a part of the new world.

You have been trained to believe your joy is dependent upon something outside of yourself, that you are *not* sovereign. Once you shift your perception, your vibratory level will rise, and you will gain access to the desires you have held that you have yet to see come to fruition.

There is great *power* in your perception. Do it in your knowing and belief, and release any shred of victimization energy that has held you captive.

Go forward, go forward, go forward!

Don't stop. Don't turn around, and don't follow anyone.

You Are a Creator

For the universe to deliver, it has to feel the vibratory connection between what you believe, what you are aligned to, and what you present. When you align to a belief in yourself, you present that energy to the universe, and the universe will deliver on it.

If you are unaligned with what you are presenting, the universe cannot deliver to the false character you are portraying.

So it is for you to know yourself.

What do I want to feel?

Is what I want going to provide me with that feeling?

Sometimes what you think you want isn't going to bring you the feeling of what you want. Instead of clinging to a specific idea, trust that the universe will bring you the feeling of what you want. Try to remain open to the possibility that things could come to you in a way other than the one you're thinking or even hoping they will. The universe sees further out than your present moment, so quite possibly it will detect any potential changes or shifts in you that may change your perception of what you are wanting in the present moment. In some sense, it's always one step (or ten) ahead of you.

You have to become what you want in order to get what you want. You cannot look to the masses to give it to you. You have to feel it and embody it and then convey that to the universe so it can supply you with a feeling that will *fill* you, not one that satisfies others' desires and will leave you empty.

To become what you want, you have to create what you want.

You are creators. You can't ever *stop* being a creator. You cannot stop because every time you have a thought or a feeling, you create. It is what you do every moment of every day. There is no escaping it. Whenever you are looking at, thinking about, or doing something, you are creating because both your human and source are experiencing. You could lie in your bed all day, going nowhere, and you would still be experiencing based upon how you were feeling as you were lying there.

There are two ways that creating can feel. It can feel effortless or difficult. Both will yield you a result, but how you obtain that result can make the creating process less joyful.

If you choose difficult, we'll tell you why: you love a good story to tell. You love to create a character for others to view that seems unattainable. Now they value you because of your struggle, and through the eyes of others, now you can value yourself.

You don't have to create through struggle. You can create through ease, but you have to recognize the choice you have.

You can create your own universe, and everything about it can be designed by you from start to finish. You are the picker, the chooser, and the one who decides what to believe and what to add to the universe that is you.

Chapter 2

HOW DOES THE
UNIVERSE WORK?

UNDERSTANDING HOW THE UNIVERSE works is important for
humans. Eventually an understanding comes where you know
that all things being experienced are necessary for each person
and that you can have compassion for them as you allow them
to play out.

Notice areas in your life that are going to be problematic
or cause you to have a negative emotional response. Eventually
you can decide to give up the detrimental behavior because it
begins to feel worse than allowing the situation to play out as it
is and experience it. Even though they're not necessarily wanted
or liked, it will feel worse for you to try to contain them, remove
them, or fix them.

When the shift happens, humans can be surprised that they
don't need to control what others are doing. They don't have to
tell them what to do. They simply know what they want, and
they also know that if the other person doesn't align to it, they

will very naturally part or drift away. There doesn't have to be a big, drama-filled exit. Instead, they honor themselves, and they will feel their energy system withdraw from the one they are not in alignment with. They realize that all they need to do is choose what they want in their sovereignty because they know what feels good to them and what they want.

3D, 4D, and 5D

3D, 4D, and 5D are simply descriptions of the level of consciousness you're in. In 3D, there is little involvement of your soul—you are consumed by separateness because of scarcity, fear, and victimization. These dense, lower vibrational emotions are a part of 3D consciousness. At 5D, you are at a high vibrational level, fully connected with the source. 4D is the transitional place where humans go as they move up and down from 3D to 5D. No one goes right from 3D into 5D; they keep gradually shifting, going up and down, and each time gaining a little more understanding of how they create a more elevated consciousness.

Everyone is at a different level. However, during the current transitional period, more and more humans are shifting into the higher levels of consciousness. This transitional period is 4D, as humans begin to know that change is coming. This change is humans realizing they create, understanding that nothing random is happening, and eliminating victimization.

People are beginning to realize they are the ones drawing experiences to themselves.

They aren't doing it on their own, though. They are doing it because of the oneness with the rest of humanity. The earth is an all-inclusive resort. Everything that is focused on is added to it, and nothing can be taken back. That is because as we choose, as we feel, and as we emit emotion, the universe responds immediately by expanding into it. So all that has been added by your population for wanting more peace, more love, and more unity is what is creating higher levels of consciousness. At the same time, many of you would say, "Well, there has been so much conflict, war, racism, and poverty." We would say we have transmuted it all to love. All the energy we, the source, receive is risen. When are you going to do the same by choosing love instead of hate?

You, too, can transmute energy by picking the higher-vibration responses and by knowing there is no good or bad, or right and wrong, and that you have become better because of all you have contributed. Learn the lessons that are mirrored back to you from all you are in interaction with rather than opposing them. This is what will speed the change you are all wanting.

As more of the oneness starts to shift in a higher direction toward 5D, it automatically pulls the rest of the group with them. There will be a few that are stuck in the old way, but they will feel uncomfortable because the new resonance is the dominant collective consciousness way. As the levels of consciousness get higher and higher, there will be less and less negativity or bad events happening because humans will have the awareness they are creating them and will begin to create differently.

We are moving from 3D to 5D reality. We want you to understand what this means and how you are affected by this transition.

You're not leaving the earth in 5D; you are expanding your consciousness, where you will reside in the higher tones of love, creation, manifestation, and well-being. You cannot stay in this vibratory level (5D) if you are in negativity—you will be shaken off.

We want you to understand that this transitional period will have its trying moments. At first, you won't quite fit into 5D, so you may go back and complete a few things at the 4D (and possibly 3D) level of consciousness. It's natural to bounce between what you used to believe and what you have now become. We don't want you condemning yourself for the lower vibratory emotions you bounce back to because this is the process.

As you accept this truth, then you will become the embodiment of source. Your source is love. Your source is not a contrived expectation of perfection.

As you gain this new, 5D consciousness, you will pop in and out of new self-awareness. As you pop out, you'll go back down to scarcity, fear, and victimization, lower vibrational emotions. Some of you will take this very hard. You will say, "I know better. Why do I keep falling back to 3D?"

As you judge yourself for not embodying the new consciousness, however, you will wash yourself in the old consciousness and re-create (or regurgitate) old patterns, thoughts, and behaviors. We keep telling you to love and accept yourself, whatever you are experiencing. Never forget the creator you are wherever you are, so stop condemning—unless you want to create more condemnation. The only way to increase your vibratory level is through love and acceptance of yourself.

The universe is like a duplicating machine. As you live your life, you observe yourself in combination with all aspects of the universe that are all doing the same. You are the universe; you are a part of all that is. Experience yourself as all things, and as you express yourself and have preferences, the universe will reflect that back to you. You are the universe perceiving itself so it can know itself.

How can you perceive the universe in a way that will serve *you*?

Know that it *is* you. Think about how you feel about yourself and know this is the only way the universe can receive you.

Do you love yourself?

Do you honor yourself?

Do you feel safe and provided for?

Or are you afraid, unsure, and untrusting of the universe?

You are the universe you think is outside of yourself. It is *in* you. It is part of you, and it is responding *to* you.

When you accept this, you will begin to notice the things and ideas you attach to (or believe in) that do not serve you. We call this the self-analysis of self-awareness.

It's important you don't approach this self-analysis from a place of condemnation. Think of it as house cleaning. When you have a behavior you don't like, we want you to think, *I'm so happy I can see I'm moving away from what I'm wanting.* This way, you don't stand in judgment of yourself; you are simply noticing what isn't contributing to the success you want and moving away from it.

Most humans do it backward. When they notice something they don't like about themselves, they stand in judgment of it. They condemn themselves for it. The human tool starts to feel worse and worse and *worse*, and its vibratory level lowers. They begin to move further away from what they want.

Recognizing when something doesn't feel good is *good*—provided you release judgment of it. Notice it, and then move beyond it. Choose differently, and then *proceed* differently.

"Thank you, human tool, for noticing. Now we are going to move in a different direction because you noticed."

Then thank the universe and move on.

You Are Never Alone

The universe knows you personally because it is you. You are unique in every thought you have, situation you encounter, and conclusion you draw.

You are never alone because you are connected to the source, and when you become connected to the source, the source becomes you. When this happens, you'll experience an ease and have a dialogue with the source, even while conscious. When you begin to experience conscious living, your loneliness *evaporates* because there is so much communication going on between you and all that you are.

We're not saying humans can't couple for the right reasons and that it can't be enjoyable. But there are many who are coupling and it *isn't* enjoyable—this is something we would not recommend because it is ruining your own vibration levels, and you won't be able to ride to 5D and manifest what you want.

You hold a signal that is unique to you and all you have experienced. Each time you feel, the high part of you becomes greater from that signal, that vibration, and that tone that is unique to you.

No two humans are ever alike, nor could they ever be.

You are the unique culmination of everything you have ever experienced.

How could that be a mistake?

How could that be forsaken?

How could this universe ever keep track of every emanation that fills worlds upon worlds?

You, however, are keeping track of yourself. You are an emanation of the source, and your emanation is unique, with its own unique energy signal. No one will ever have the same thought even if they have the exact same experience (but no two experiences are ever alike). Some humans try to deny their uniqueness by copying others. This skews their signal, and because the universe knows who you really are, it cannot deliver to you when your signal is scrambled.

Your signal becomes scrambled when you emanate something that is different than what you truly feel, i.e., hiding or pretending to be something you are not causes disconnection. It is so important to live in your authentic true nature. Many will say, "I can't let that out. I can't be who I really am." They use the one in front of them as their excuse for scrambling their own signal. The hard truth is no one scrambles your signal but you.

All of you are unique—all of you matter, create, and *allow* the universe to know itself in unlimited ways. You are a part of all that is: source, god, and the universe.

The Universe Is Expansion

Your unique signal is expanding consciousness with your view of itself.

Every person or entity, as it is experiencing, is becoming *more* because they are experiencing. This is why the universe is never-ending and why it keeps going and going and going internally. That's what expansion is: the cumulation of every experience by everything that exists.

Think of a library. It can only hold so much material, and if more material is added, it needs to expand. It's the same with the universe. In fact, the expansion of the universe is being proved by science today.

For example, look back at yourself as a child. Do you see the difference between your consciousness when you came to the earth and your consciousness now? And you still have years of expansion left.

Now imagine the magnitude of expansion that occurs in endless lifetimes over endless galaxies.

Every time you experience anything, you expand to the highest vibration as it is transmuted in the frequency of love. You provide feedback to all that is about those experiences.

We don't care if you expand through negative or positive experiences. Either way, all that is, is expanded. This earth is for your enjoyment. It's for *you* to go after your mission. The reason you came to the earth is to manifest as the source, rise above the density that experience was created in, and become the light you have expanded to because of each experience you had while in your human form.

This is why we tell you never to regret a negative experience. However horrific it was, that experience has been transmuted by you for *you*. Your ability to move away from the experience and love yourself for having made a deposit to the source is what is going to align you to what you desire. You expand the moment you have a desire, but alignment will bring it in form because it is you aligning to your source where it already is. We, in all that is, are transmuters of energetic charges that come in the form of emotion, and then those charges are raised to the highest energetic level of love. You, in your human mastery or understanding of this concept, can choose to do the same the minute you feel negativity. You can decide to gain from the experiences whatever lessons they hold rather than resorting to victimization and remaining in the low charge that they originated in.

The Universe Is Contrast

The universe understands you, accepts you, and becomes you. It is the pure positive energy of love. It comes in love and uses the incarnation of the human to experience itself in form, but it must withstand great contrast as it enters the density of your reality.

If this is accomplished, the result is a rising out of the 3D vibrational level. Contrast is what causes a change to the existing dimensional level. As contrast is resolved and the vibratory level rises, there is more love, less fear, more understanding, quicker manifestations, and rebalancing.

Contrast is the key to expansion.

That doesn't mean you have to go against the contrast current rather than allow it to pull you along with ease. Whenever you go through periods of resistance, know this is transformation energy. It is what sets you up or puts you in the exact feeling for effortless change.

Why are you experiencing negativity when someone in your

life does something you don't like? Because you have a preference in how you want to feel and a way you want to see your life and experiences. Your preference is what's causing your growth and expansion.

Many of you go against yourself and get stuck in negative emotions instead of riding the wave and allowing it to bring you to shore. Every time you experience a way of being that is unaligned, your work is done. You have expanded by your preference. You have already become that thing you say you want:

- If only I could be famous.

- If only I could have so much money.

- If only I could have this or that.

You are experiencing the feeling of having everything you have ever dreamed of in all that is. You are satisfied, fulfilled, and expanded in every experience you've had.

The only reason you struggle on the earth is because you get stuck in the experience. You refuse to release it and use the expansion for what it was intended. You've already become it—your work is done. You don't need to keep re-experiencing it. You can, if you don't move on, and you'll expand more and more. But how can you have an easier human experience? Choose it. Decide that every time you have what you deem a "negative emotion," your source is calling you—begging you—to take a look at what has occurred. Know that how you are choosing to look at it is the cause of the negativity you are feeling. To consciously live your life, choose good-feeling reactions to your experiences rather than becoming the experience and staying in the negativity.

Simply be grateful for the experience and allow the contrast to find you so that you may know yourself.

When you do that, you expand to the greater version of what you have experienced. If you have experienced extreme sadness and loneliness, you have expanded to extreme *happiness* and *fulfillment*. As you move into admiration and gratitude, you can pull yourself away from the contrast because you have aligned yourself to a higher level of consciousness. Then you can experience what contrast has given you. Experience the contrast. Feel the emotion, and then leave it. If you continue to stay at a low vibratory level, you will attract more low vibratory experiences. Instead, feel the emotion and then move to a higher state of consciousness in order to *attract* higher states of consciousness. That is how you bring your desires to you.

However, know that you can't force this process. Sometimes it takes time to move out of a negative energy pattern. You may be at the brink of breaking through one, so you are going to feel it quite strongly. You need to sit in it for a while so it can make its way to the surface and then out of you. You need to trust the process.

We recently spoke to someone who has something she's wanted to manifest for a long time. She has wanted it *a lot* for a long time. We explained to her that as she moves in the energy of not having it she *becomes* the frustration she feels; therefore, the universe provides her with frustration. When something takes longer than you want it to, you have to *trust*. You need to get into a state of joy, one that allows you to accept that what you're experiencing right now is what is needed for your well-being, growth, and expansion.

You must always be hyper-aware of how *you* are feeling because that is how the universe feels you. If you feel devalued, you will be devalued. If you feel frustrated, you will be provided with frustration. If you feel not good enough, you'll be treated as not good enough. You need to move yourself into an emotive value you want returned to you.

If you try to force yourself to be different, to be better, or to change, you will only create more contrast. If this is the case, perhaps you need more expansion.

Don't judge it.

Don't decide you've done something wrong.

There is no rubbish being created. You are a creator, the source, a god. You have desire and know what you're doing. It takes a certain amount of contrast to get what you want. You're going to keep creating and experience contrast until the day you leave this plane.

Contrast as a Springboard

Many spiritual books try to soothe you and tell you you'll never feel bad again. We say that if you never feel bad again, you aren't living!

You need that contrast to create what you want, so smile at the contrasting experience rather than condemn yourself for the experience. You will always, *always*, rise because of it—provided you don't *become* it.

"I'm a terrible husband."

"I'm a terrible father."

"I'm unhealthy."

"I'm not where I should be."

This is not the route to where you want to go.

If you focus on your poor habits, shortcomings, and judgment and condemnation of yourself, you can never become a wonderful version from the contrast you experienced.

Use the contrast as a springboard, something to jump off from and propel you to where you want to go. This is how you become the best possible version of yourself: love yourself for your experiences. Know they are calling you, guiding you, and bringing you to *you*.

Whatever you focus on you will create. If you keep focusing on the wrongdoing of others, you will not create what you want for yourself.

Justifications and Opposition

Be careful.

Don't push against. Don't argue, and don't start opposing those who think differently from you. Instead, perceive your preference and allow others their own. Not doing so is a trap many of you fall into, and you feel justified as you do it.

There is never a time when a human feels more justified than when someone is doing something they deem as wrong—especially when it comes to spirituality. The human wants to present their opinion immediately. As they judge someone's ignorance, *they* have become ignorant.

You have to reach the understanding that you may be on a planet with billions of people, but every single one of them is a sovereign being. Your opinion doesn't matter *at all* to them and how they create. It only matters to you and how you create. The only way *you* can create is when you're focused on what *you* would like to see in the world and what you would like your addition to be to all that is. When you do, beings with similar interests, ways of thinking, and thoughts will be attracted to you.

You don't get what you want to see by focusing on those who are not doing what you think they should be doing. When you do that, you will only create more of them.

There may be a time when you witness blatant racism, for instance. Understand you have called that person to yourself. Release the urge to judge them. Release any feelings of aggravation, and move on.

We understand this is a hard concept. You can't help thinking you're right and they're wrong.

This is how trouble begins.

Understand that opposing opinions are what's needed to support the conclusion you have come to for yourself. That's it—that's all it is. When you start to look at it this way, opposition and justification will become a thing of your past. You will know that each being is sovereign. Each has a choice, and no one has to agree with each other. There is no right and wrong—only choices and agreements to those choices.

We bet you are riled up right now. You love your right and wrong and your justifications. You are probably thinking of all the ways *we* could be wrong and *you* could be right.

We would ask you: how do you feel thinking like that at this moment?

We bet it feels controlling, dominating, and superior.

"But what about racism? What about poverty? What about abuses in every form?" you're asking.

We would tell you that you cannot change something by opposing it. As you oppose, you enter the same energy of what you are opposing through your opposition.

So what do you do?

Be that which you want to see in the world. Be an example of love, acceptance, understanding, and unity. Watch how the masses respond to that energy.

This is the only way to create the world you all say you want. Yet you continue to go about it by judging and opposing those who are not living their lives the way you would like them to.

When you meet someone in love, acceptance, and understanding, they align to the perception you're holding and very easily match your tone. Once they match your tone, all of your perceptions start to flow to them. Now they can actually become more because you have thrown them a lifeline. You don't save someone who is drowning by continually telling them to learn how to swim. You have to teach them to swim. Show; don't tell.

It is going to take some discipline in order for you to adopt this new way of being. If you have been opinionated for a long time, you're going to have a lot of contrast coming from those who have been under your influence. We're talking about you who always thinks you're right and tells others how they should think, act, and create. If you've tried to remove the sovereignty of others and force them to follow the sovereignty of *you*, then you are going to find that you attract people who oppose you because they are never going to give up their sovereignty. They're never going to be at peace with you, and you're never going to be at peace with them or yourself. You'll find conflict at every turn. The longer you've lived in this energy, the longer it will take for you to turn it around because you have justified forcing your sovereignty on others. No one will change because you are forcing them to change. All that you will find coming to you from the universe is more and more of those that you feel need changing.

Ask yourself if it feels good when others try to force their opinions and ideas on you. We know the answer is no. It doesn't feel good when you force your opinions on others either—not to them or to yourself. If this feels bad to everyone involved, how do you think the universe is going to react to it? How will it decide you want to be perceived? It will think that you want conflict, trouble, and drama in your life and provide it to you.

You need to shift out of that energy and move your attractive quality to something else. This takes time and effort because there will be some lag time, some stragglers from your previous energy. There will be those who will come in your experience to test you to see if you have truly moved out of opposition energy. Once you have made the shift, you will know by the people who surround you. Resist correcting those you think need correcting because they are only there to test you. Smile to yourself and say, "I am a sovereign being," and then let them be.

Exactly Where You Need to Be

Everything that comes out of your mouth—even if you don't necessarily agree with it—holds a vibratory level to the creation of you. Be very mindful about what you verbalize. If you constantly worry about random events happening to you, you are going to attract those experiences that provide the same feelings to you. The universe wants to give you what you want. If you continuously talk about things being hard, it will believe that you want hard things and will provide them.

Every phrase or word has a vibrational tone to it based not only on your thoughts and feelings but on the masses' use of it as well. What could the word "hard" align to? What could the transmission of the word, which encompasses all of the thoughts and feelings of those who have used it before you, align to or pull to you?

It's about awareness. Be aware of what words you are using aloud *and* in your thoughts because they will attract that vibrational tone to you.

You don't have to be perfect at this. Look at the process with appreciation and gratitude.

"I just caught myself thinking about how hard things are. I now know how easy I would like them to be. Now that I am aware of it, I can move on and replace that thought with what I really want."

Sometimes this can create that springboard effect. As you think these old thoughts, you will drop down into 3D, but by being aware, you will spring back up to 4D and then 5D.

As you practice this awareness, when you drop down into 3D, it will become so turbulent and uncomfortable that you can't stay there as long, and you'll spring back up faster and faster.

Remember, there is nothing wrong. There is nothing bad or threatening happening. There are only emotions and responses to your life experiences, and they won't harm you as long as you don't attach yourself to them.

Let the universe respond in love to the higher, greater creation you've become by the life experiences you have contributed to all that is.

When expansion occurs, it means you made a decision in your physical form and your source received it. Once you start to love yourself, you will rise a little in your human tool, and you will be able to connect to the high part of yourself.

As you gain this new awareness, you will realize you are deciding to choose. You don't have to have everything that's circling you. Instead, you can pick the things you want, the things that feel good to you and that you *want* to perceive in order to become. This is how you create.

When are you going to make the shift? When are you going to take the leap and give up fear?

We keep telling you that you are the one who chooses. Choose wisely. Don't perceive the world in fear and give up your power.

We will catch you if you jump, and then you will have proven to yourself that there is a universe that is you. There is a force far greater than what you are perceiving in your physical form, but you have to choose it. You have to perceive it in the way you want to feel.

All of your experiences will bring you to exactly where you need to be.

Chapter 3

WHAT IS MANIFESTATION?

WHAT IS MANIFESTATION?

Manifestation is when the human tool holds a resonance or its focus long enough upon anything wanted or unwanted, and then it materializes in a form that matches the resonance or focus.

Through the love of self and acceptance of the knowledge you are an experiencer who connects to the higher part of yourself, energy is transformed into exactly what you want from the experience you had. The minute you have a desire—"I don't like this. I like this, and it's what I want instead"—your higher self expands to it. You manifest the moment you have a thought.

However, as a human, you can get lodged in your tool when you stay in an emotive state where you regurgitate over and over what you don't want and stay in that lower energy state. We were asked by a client, "Why can't you create from positivity? Why must you create from negativity?" Negativity is an indicator of the distance between you the human and your higher self in a given area or topic. It may not be that your entire vibratory level is affected, but maybe your vibratory level in relationships is poor, while in your work life, you manifest very well. This means you have a lot of contrast in your relationships.

That contrast is not necessarily negative if you can understand that the universe is notifying you that you are expanding. The more contrast you experience, the bigger your expansion gets. But you'll continue to receive contrast if you don't move out of that lower vibratory level in this area. Contrast means you are stuck in your human tool and regenerating similar experiences over and over again. Yes, you are growing and expanding because of it, but the expansion is getting so far ahead of where you are lodged as a human that the contrast is becoming uncomfortable.

Manifestation Misconceptions

Manifestation is not "pie in the sky." You can't say, "I want a $10 million home tomorrow and the money to support it," because you don't have belief that it is possible. The people who say this are simply running their mouths because they read they can have anything they want, but they have no idea how manifestation is actually achieved.

You have to be able to perceive and believe in what you're asking for. If you're currently living in a $500,000 home, you could look at $750,000—maybe even $1 million if you have great belief—and think, *I can get myself there*. You need to move your belief up incrementally; inch it up a little at a time.

It's like reaching for a book on a shelf. You'll never reach it if you're ten feet away, but if you're on your tippy toes and grazing it, you can push yourself and reach that book. It's the same for manifestation. You can't set the bar so high it's not believable. You have to keep it within the range of what's reasonable for your current belief and perception levels. If you push your manifestation too far, it'll have the reverse effect because you'll feel so far away from it, so self-defeated, that you'll move further away from it.

Possibilities and Probabilities

What are the possibilities and probabilities of your life?

Well, we would ask you, what have you thought about, and how often have you thought about it?

Every thought you have ever had (and will have) is now a possibility in your life. Every probability is a possibility that you have added emotion to. Emotion is the fuel that causes more and more thoughts surrounding the probability, causing it to become a belief in you.

You are not nearly diligent enough in the creation of possibilities and even *less* diligent in the creation of *probabilities*. You ignore your guidance system, which alerts you to what you create.

The universe feels you notice something. It is added to your universe, and then you have experiences based on what you have added *and* how closely your vibration matches the add. If you continue to hold the same resonance, emotions will start to accumulate to support what you have added. As that happens, thoughts will intensify in frequency, and things will begin to take form. You will say, "It's true. I see what I observed and what I felt. I believe it, and now it is reality."

How passionate you feel will be the determining factor for when your physical manifestation will be formed.

Every time you are unconscious of what your guidance system is trying to tell you, you will create by default. If you are unaware of how you feel, you will have no way of knowing what is about to happen next. Emotions are your indicator that a probability is close to becoming a reality. It could be a positive emotion for a positive reality or a negative emotion for a negative reality. Both signal where you've been holding your focus and are now creating form.

As you think about your manifestation over and over and over again and those emotions get stronger, they act as a notification from all that is that your manifestation is coming and is about to reach you. It can reach you in positivity, or it can reach you in negativity, depending on what you are focused upon. During this ramping-up period, there does come a point of recognition. In the case of negativity, this is often when a human reaches the "breaking point," when you can't take anymore and you realize that the situation is out of control. At this point, the probability of manifestation is close, but you have a choice. You always have the free will to readjust or move away from what you have been adding to your focus.

If something really good is coming, you get an excited feeling. Prior to us arriving, Robin had a lot of focus on, and was extremely interested in, channelers. She didn't know how it would happen, but she could feel the coming of it. How? Because she had read so many books about channeling, she knew that experiencing a Kundalini rising was a prerequisite, and she had already had that experience. There were enough confirming factors in her experience that she started to truly believe. She perceived so many things pointing in the channeling direction that the feeling of probability started to become a reality. Once something we are perceiving becomes fueled by emotions, it becomes believable, and form (or the reality of it) is soon to follow. A human will also sense when a manifestation is close by the rising desire they have for it. All of these things are working together: perceiving, believing, and, finally, receiving.

The universe is a duplicating machine—it will not judge you; it will not interfere with you. It will simply reflect back to you. You can arm yourself with the knowledge of how you create, and you can intentionally create by controlling your focus. You can pick what you focus on and pay attention to how often you think about what you've chosen to focus on. Then feel the emotions as what you've chosen to focus on begins to transform from a possibility to a probability.

Anything that you focus on, which then gets added to your universe, is a possibility. Probabilities are the possibilities you've chosen and added emotion to, which are then focused on over and over and over again. If I say, "We may go to town," no one will be disappointed if we don't go because it was just a possibility. If I say, "We're going to town," people will want to know why we aren't because it's probably meant to be.

Possibilities are a passing thought or a gentle noticing. For instance, someone passes by with beautiful brown hair and you think, *I like brown hair.* That's a possibility. However, perhaps your husband notices women with brown hair, and you don't like that.

Now every time a woman with brown hair walks by, you look at your husband and wonder if he's noticing. Now you've added the emotions to the possibility, and it's a probability. (Remember, a possibility is more of a noticing or a passing thought. Probabilities are related to the passing thought, but there are emotions attached to them now.) Each time you feel uncomfortable and devalued. All of these build up the emotion, and once the emotion is felt, the creative process has been shifted and is starting to generate power. Now it will be difficult for you to take your eyes off the next brunette who comes along, and they will because you've added emotion and energy into that possibility and turned it into a probability. There's a difference between liking brown hair and feeling vulnerable to someone with brown hair.

Once you have intentionally chosen things that make you feel *good*, the universe can assist you by making it easier and easier for you by duplicating thoughts you've chosen to support your focus.

This is what a master does.

Masters don't create by default—they create by understanding: *I choose. I feel, and the universe matches me.*

Nothing random is happening—nothing by luck. What you focus on is returned to you in the form of more thoughts. More thoughts create emotions, and emotions manifest into form.

You are the master, chooser, picker, and *creator* of everything you perceive in your life.

It's important, however, to never deny the emotion or feeling you are having because it was an experience that was needed. You will never have an experience that is not for your betterment, even if it doesn't feel good or seem that way. Emotions are never good or bad. Instead, acknowledge the emotion, and then soothe yourself out of it.

Don't tell yourself, "I don't want to be feeling this. I don't want to be thinking about this." Use appreciation. For instance, you're driving in rush hour traffic, and someone tries to cut you off. You feel a burst of anger. It's okay to feel that anger, but don't hold on to it. Feel it. Acknowledge it, and then release it. Be like a screen door and let the emotion slide right out of you. And understand that that driver cut you off because your energy drew him to you. Never forget that you attract every experience to yourself. Unless you want to run into that on the highway on a regular basis, you need to clear it out of your vibration. Decide that when you go out for a drive, everything always goes well. You meet nice people who drive carefully, and you never have any problems. Tell yourself this every time you drive to pre-pave a nice experience for yourself. By focusing on these good things, you raise your vibration level, and that's what you'll attract. If you get in your car while rushed or angry and don't focus on raising that level, you'll attract poor driving experiences. Instead, take a moment to adjust your focus and set a new intention for how you want your drive to go.

Energy Can Be Recouped

There is a flow of energy to every human, but that energy level can vary based upon how you are deciding to view your experiences. Choosing to give can replenish your energy and make you feel as though you have more to give.

However, you have to be careful what you expend your energy on. What you expend your energy on is going to bring something to you. If you expend it on something of value to you or through an act of kindness, then you will bring to yourself something of value.

We know that it can be a little disheartening for humans to hear that they have inadvertently added negative situations to their universe that are now spinning around them. But as you educate yourself and grow, you don't have to revisit the things that are spinning around out in your universe—provided you don't lower yourself back down to that level and then hang out there.

The Case of the Yellow Sweatshirt

If you want to show your human self how manifestation works, ask to see something silly. This is a great tool that humans can use. Pose something ridiculous to yourself, and then focus upon it in fun, laughter, and knowing belief. Name anything that you want the universe to show you, and in short order, it will show you.

We recently had Robin try this, and she asked to see a yellow sweatshirt. She asked the universe to show her a yellow sweatshirt, and then she focused on it periodically for a few days. She watched to see one everywhere she went and wondered how it would arrive. A few days later, on a call with her editor, Robin was telling her about the manifestation game, and the editor squealed in glee before turning on her camera. She was wearing a bright yellow sweatshirt that she had bought the day before. Robin was thrilled because she had received her manifestation in the perfect way. She hadn't wanted to own a yellow sweatshirt, and the universe knew that. So it provided the perfect manifestation: a yellow sweatshirt that she didn't have to wear.

This is how the universe works. It's funny, magical, and responsive. It will prove itself to you. And if you start proving manifestation works to yourself in small ways, you can incrementally begin increasing what you want to manifest. Ask for a yellow sweatshirt to start, and once it shows up, you can ask for something a little more valuable and unique. Each time you receive your request, you can ask for a little bit more until you're manifesting the huge desires you want with no effort and little lag. Think of it as building your manifestation muscle. The more you use this muscle (the belief that you'll receive what you ask for), the easier it is to lift heavier desires.

How quickly you receive your manifestation will depend on your vibration level. The speed of your manifestation is a great indicator of how you're feeling.

Let's look at another metaphor to ensure that you are really understanding manifestation belief. Imagine you go to the store, purchase a space heater, take it home, and plug it in. Power comes through the plug and into the heater, and the heater heats up the room. As a human, you have to plug yourself into the energy source and believe that you can heat up the room. Believe in what you desire. Do you ever doubt that when you plug in your heater, the room will heat up? No. You know that the power is coming because you've plugged it into the energy source. You cannot be wishy-washy about your belief and get the result you're looking for.

Believe Anything Is Possible

Set an intention for anything you want to attract. For instance, if you're unpacking boxes from a move and you realize you need thumbtacks, take a moment to set an intention to find them. With belief and an intention, you'll find them on the top of the next box. You can even find a container of money this way. However, many can't believe that's possible, and that lack of belief is what's holding them separate from the manifestation. You have no problem believing that you can find a container of thumbtacks, but you can't believe you'll find a container full of money.

Why is that? Is it because you don't feel you should be that "lucky" or because tacks are run of the mill? The truth is that everything that you come into contact with is run of the mill. You are choosing to believe that some manifestations are difficult while others are not.

Think of the human who thinks, *I'm going to work really hard. I'm going to make it happen.* Then they work really hard, but they don't make it happen. Now they feel frustrated and judge themselves: *I'm not going to get what I want.* This moves them in the opposite direction of where they want to go. This is forced action. Instead, they could have known what they wanted and understood that it has to be funded through the source. They don't worry about how it's going to happen or try to orchestrate it. Inspired action will happen automatically. When you need to have action, you will *know* it. You won't be able to miss it. Inspired action will be orchestrated by all that is, not by your human tool. You are here to pick and choose your desires and then let the universe do its job to bring them to you.

Remember that you are the universe, and the universe is you. When you decide you want something or that something makes you feel a certain way, the universe then conspires to bring you in form what will match that feeling. There is you as the human, and there is also you as the source, which is a flow of consciousness that is inclusive of you and everything you see. As you have your desires, your universe changes and becomes inclusive of your desires.

Separation

It is not for us to govern how you live your life. It is for you to determine how you feel as you live. Your feeling and determination of your experience is the deciding factor on how the universe responds to you.

How do you feel in your interactions with others? Do you perceive them in love or in *separation?*

Separation is anything that is not love.

Separation is you moving away from the high part of yourself, experiencing the charge of negativity, not recognizing it as the message it is, and then continuing to separate until negative experiences begin showing up. You may only be separating in one category of your life, or you may be separating in many. But as this separation grows, the amount of contrast will also grow with it in hopes of getting you to recognize that this separation is happening. As you get stuck in your human and stay in your negativity, your higher self is growing bigger and bigger and bigger. Eventually—and the whole reason the universe has set it up this way—you won't be able to tolerate that discomfort anymore. You'll feel worse and worse until it drives you to the point that you have to recognize what you've done, how far you've separated, and come back to your higher self. The good news is that all of that suffering created big growth, and you'll reap the benefits of it. Nothing is lost.

For example, say someone wants to become famous. You're working, working, working, but you're not getting it, not getting it, not getting it. Your energy is building more and more, and then all of a sudden, you decide you are not going to try anymore. You feel lost: "I put all this effort in. Where did it go?" It didn't go anywhere. It's all in your universe waiting for you. Now you decide to open a new business, and guess what. You're excited about this new desire that's going to fulfill you. Your higher self meets you in that excited energy, and you never saw any of this coming. All of that energy you were using to become famous comes rushing back in, and your business is a huge success.

The effort you put into the world will always return to you. It's like a boomerang. Where humans get caught up is in feeling discouraged. You feel let down that you didn't get the thing you thought you should because of the effort you put in. Always remember that all of your effort and energy doesn't go away. It's recirculating. The moment you decide to align, you're getting paid.

There is no waste of time; there is no wrong path to take. Everything is building and accumulating—and it's all yours. Every experience you've had is yours, and no one can take it away from you. Even if something doesn't work out for you, even if you take a different path, you will never lose anything that you have deposited into your universe. And that energy can be used for whatever you decide to use it for.

If you perceive in separation, you are going to continue to experience situations that will cause you to justify being separated.

Why would you ever want to justify not feeling good?

Why would you consciously choose to not feel good?

Because you are not choosing consciously—you are *un*consciously living in the belief that someone else is to blame for how you feel. No one chooses how you feel but you. No one can evoke something within you that is not already actively a part of you.

If you have to continue to defend, justify, and be validated, the universe is revealing something you are missing.

But what could you be missing?

You are worthy. You are enough. You are loved.

If you already felt worthy, that you were enough and were loved, this is all you would receive. If you feel unworthy, if you feel as though you are not enough, and if you feel unloved, that is what your experiences will reveal to you.

Why would you ever be mad at someone who is only the reflection of what you are?

If you feel unworthy, you will attract those who also feel you are unworthy. When you move to defense, anger, resentment, and hate, you become a victim who has no self-awareness of the one thing you are: a creator of your own experience.

Everyone, everything, and every *experience* you have is yours. Start being pleasant. Start being kind. Start making your own creation *your* fault. When you experience something you can't let go of or something you don't feel good as you experience it, *own* it and change how you see it. Get the messages that the messengers have for you. Every experience you have, good, bad, or otherwise, is a reflection of what you have chosen and put in your universe and have then attracted to yourself based on your vibratory level.

Nothing will come to you that you do not bring to yourself. Make it your life's mission to love your life and be accountable for all you experience.

Delight in those who show you the truth of who you are.

Delight in all your experiences, and know they are your creation.

Delight in transforming your life into exactly what you believe.

Once you understand *you* are doing specific things that cause you to not get what you want at the speed you want it, you can start to adjust how you choose to live your life.

Learn How to Operate Your Tool

You keep saying...

"Well, I *am* fat."

"I did lose my money."

"My wife left me."

We say, when you see yourself as fat, as you see yourself as poor, and as you see yourself as unloved, this is what the universe responds to. In order to change and obtain mastery, you *must* master your mind.

In all three of these statements, you have attached yourself to the human, your tool. Instead, learn to operate the tool. Use your focus to retrain it, and then let the tool manifest the results based on your focus.

You Are an Energy Transmitter

You are an energy transmitter. By the emission of your feelings to all that is, you are creating.

In opposition energy, you cannot create what you want—instead, you prevent manifestations from occurring. Opposition stops joy, prevents peace, and grinds energy to a stop. It eventually turns in the opposite direction of where you want to go.

You are here to accept yourself, love yourself, and create a reflection of you for all the world to see. As you move into acceptance and love of self, you can move toward peace, which results in pure joy and bliss.

Now you are in the right place to manifest!

Now you have a divine opportunity before you!

Now you can follow your soul's guidance and allow easy, perfect, and aligned manifestation to materialize in your universe!

All you need to do is focus on what brings you peace, happiness, and joy. Is it lovely music? Is it a partner? Is it a beautiful flower garden? Is it candles burning? As you set your scene and move into following your peace, happiness, and joy, the universe will surprise you with manifestations that you didn't believe were possible.

How do you want to feel?

Ask yourself this in every interaction you have. If you do not produce a feeling that will return peace, happiness, and joy to you, you are giving up your soul's desire.

Notice where you feel wonderful—follow it, hang on to it, and never give it up. Appreciate and admire the process of creation you are a part of—be grateful for it because this is the stream of consciousness that produces results.

With every cell in your body, know you are the producer, designer, and receiver of *everything* that comes to you in your life. Spend the time convincing yourself of this fact, and watch the *results* convince you even more.

Know One Thing: You Create

What is it you want to create?

Whatever it is, do it consciously. Do it well. Do it with intention.

We are not talking about pie-in-the-sky creations—we are talking about feelings, emotions, and desires.

How do you want to feel?

For some, it is important to make others believe as they believe. They cannot focus on their own feelings because they are focused on opposing everyone else's. As you oppose anything or anyone, the universe receives that opposition energy and opposes you from getting what you want.

Why is it so important that you make others be as you are? Just let go—make a decision to be sovereign and to allow others the same luxury. Decide what you want to be, and then be that. It can be so easy, so smooth, and so much more rewarding.

You must create a new, better outcome and then let go of that creation.

Many of you humans are pretty good at following physical processes and have great success in doing it. You know full well that if you want to paint your house, scraping all the loose paint and then priming the surface is going to give you the best foundation to hold the paint you place over it. Not causing yourself extra work or aggravation is important to you.

Why don't you prepare yourself mentally the same way you would paint your house?

Scrape off and remove anything that is going to cause you problems by observing yourself and how you are thinking. Start to lay down a new foundation for yourself with new ways of thinking to build upon. Now apply your thoughts to that surface. This will give you a finish you will be happy with.

Remember, you are the master and the creator of it all.

The only way you can ever make things better is to *be better*. Be the manifestations you desire.

In your denial of another's experience, you have given up your own. It is a waste of your time to judge others; it is a waste of your time to try to be right. Experience and decide for yourself what you want to see in the world by keeping your focus on it. That is how you manifest.

Chapter 4

DO YOU PRACTICE SELF-LOVE?

WHAT IS SELF-LOVE?

Self-love is loving yourself for coming to this earth, having the human experiences you are having, and expanding all that is because of them. It is knowing that you are worthy, you are enough, just by that endeavor. Nobody is keeping track, judging you, or deciding whether or not you have value by what you experience. The only person who does that to you is yourself, and that is not self-love.

Self-love knows that it is an experiencer. An experiencer is one who is perceiving circumstances, situations, and things that are occurring based upon all the lives and lineages that are within them that they have ever experienced. It's not just what you have experienced in this lifetime but all the many experiences that you've already had that you don't even remember being there for.

How can you judge yourself when there is so much more to you than you know?

Why Do People Hide?

Because they become accustomed to the feedback they get for the *projection* they offer others. It makes them feel they have to modify themselves in order to be accepted by others.

The idea of hiding doesn't make a lot of sense because it simply creates more hiding. When you hide, the energy of hiding hinders you, so you begin engaging with the exact thing you don't want any part of.

When you stop hiding, however, and start being authentically, honestly you, your experience gets flooded with people who are the same. You drop the bags you didn't know you were carrying. Your arms feel lighter and freer.

We want you to drop your bags and decide you're not going to hide anymore.

Step into the power of who you are.

There are those who hide and those who encourage us to hide by their opinion or view of us. One must realize that hiding doesn't make something not exist—it creates a lie that is real.

Your reality is one that you are perceiving and others are viewing. You can have your reality be yours, or you can allow others' perception of you to create you.

We encourage all humans who feel they are not mainstream or hold a perception of themselves that is not theirs to never let another's view affect how they perceive themselves. In other words, you do you.

Misconceptions of Self-Love

The biggest misconception of self-love is that you have to do things perfectly in order to be loved. That you have to be a spiritual icon that sits in the corner all day and doesn't drink, doesn't smoke, doesn't swear, and doesn't have any fun. This is a false belief that many humans have adopted. You think there is a how-to list that one must follow in order to be worthy, and this is not true.

When we talk about self-love, we are not talking about getting a massage or taking a bubble bath. We are talking about something different. We're talking about a human deciding to love and never stand in judgment of themselves and for having experiences. When a human learns to release themself from their perception of right and wrong and simply feel the experiences life presents to them, they are practicing self-love.

In this approach, as you learn from your human experiences, you can choose how you want to emanate rather than become the human in whatever level of consciousness it is stuck in.

The Condemned Self

You are going to change. You are going to be different. You are finally going to make the shift.

The idea that you have condemned yourself is enough to ruin your plan.

Change comes in the love, acceptance, and *trust* of self. The universe fulfills your desires because it matches you in your *support* of you. It will never match you in your condemnation. It will never agree there is something about you that needs to change.

Hold your desire for yourself in love—not in judgment. Every time you flub up, continue to love, and your being will turn into that love. Your source will only respond to what you offer it. If you offer dissatisfaction of yourself, you will generate more dissatisfaction.

To remind you, separation is a lack of self-love. Humans love to justify the reasons they are unlovable. It's what you do when you become the human.

Many humans think that when they do something society deems shameful or wrong, they're going to be condemned. What they don't realize is they are condemning themselves. They have decided to believe the perception that others have placed upon them.

The universe isn't going to condemn you for what your human tool did when on earth. There's nobody standing at the altar ready to point their finger at you for a life lived. The universe is happy for all expansion, no matter what shape that expansion takes. It's happy with everything you have done. It's your human tool that is condemning and judging yourself. *You* do it all.

We keep telling you you're not the tool, yet you insist on becoming it and then *changing* it into something you can deem as worthy.

Worthiness isn't something you must obtain by some false perception of perfection. Worthiness is a perception of love.

You are pure positive love experiencing contrast in the reality you are in. Stay connected in your love, and just observe yourself in contrast. Leave out your judgment about its worthiness.

Why Must You Hang onto Things?

Why do humans hang onto things?

Do you keep all of the empty boxes of everything you order? There would be no space for anything new. It could feel overwhelming and out of control.

There's nothing there for you in the empty boxes your orders already arrived in, so throw them out and get rid of them. Stop hanging onto them as though there is still something of value inside.

The same applies to your experiences. Once you've had a negative experience, throw out the box it came in. Stop saving them up. Stop looking back inside, and stop expecting something different from what you already have received. Break down the boxes, and make room for what's coming.

You Are Connected to Love

Humans continually ignore how they feel in a given situation.

Your primary goal as a human is to create. After all, that's why you have a human tool—to experience life. You decide, through emoting, what you want to create.

How would you like to feel as you do it?

You can allow yourself to be governed by your emotions, or you can govern your emotions by picking and choosing the ones you want to feel. You have a choice and decision to make.

Ask yourself, "How do I want to feel?"

When put that way, doesn't it seem silly to pick anything that doesn't feel *good*? Yet humans tend to believe in suffering.

Instead of a focus on suffering, can you imagine the level of love you are connected to and a part of?

The closest thing we could use as an example is the love you receive from your pets. They love you and hold their view of you even when you do not. Your pets have their limits, though. Eventually, if you abuse them, they will cower and distrust you.

The love you are connected to never cowers or distrusts you. It comes from purity, so it remains firmly standing in defense and protection of you.

Love is pure. It is 100 percent pure positive energy—it is what you are connected to as a part of all it is.

We have hinted to you in past communications to ask from the universe in your purity, and this is what we are talking about. When you want something provided to you, do it from purity. There are many levels of love, but the level of love that connects to you is pure—nothing will dim it, and nothing will be withheld from it. Grasping this concept is the best way you can achieve what you are wanting.

In love of self, you become like the universe—you decide never to cower or distrust. Sometimes you think, *I am loving enough. It's good enough.* And we would say love *more.* Love your human on *all* days. Love your human in all its feelings and emotions. Trust it. Don't put judgments or limits on the life experiences you are having.

Once you become the experience, which happens when you judge and limit, your expansion stops. In love you are *un*judged and *un*limited, and nothing can inhibit that stream of energy.

Did we say anything about perfection?

Did we even say anything about doing it *better*?

We did not. We said do it in *love.* Period.

Increase Your Vibrations by Focusing on Love

Humans tell us it can feel false or inauthentic to sing a song that everything's okay when it really isn't because you're fighting with your significant other or you've lost all your money. And it's easy for us to say, "Pull up a positive thought and get yourself out of that situation you're in." You probably want to say a few choice words to us in response. We understand. If you can't find a lifting thought or anything to raise your vibratory level in that area, what you can do is focus on an area in your life where you are in alignment, where you love yourself and know that what you're doing is done well and that feels good. An area that feels in connection.

You may know that you're a good father to your children or a good husband to your spouse. But you may be struggling in your career or as a provider, and this is where the worry and doubt come in, throwing you out of alignment. When this happens, you have to take your attention off of that worry because you can't stuff something down your throat that you're not yet ready to swallow. You have to go somewhere you can swallow the good stuff, such as "I'm a good father," or "I'm a good husband." Maybe you care about the planet and take great care of your environment.

You need to bring yourself somewhere you can align yourself to love so that you can connect to your loving self. This gives you a place to go to temporarily lift your vibratory level. This moves you into connection so you can plug into your current and adjust your vibratory level enough that you can start to love yourself even in the areas of your life that aren't going well, which in turn attracts good things from the universe to those areas.

Chapter 5

HOW DO YOU
PERCEIVE?

HOW IS IT THAT YOU perceive your reality? There are many things that will cause a human to have a perception. A perception is based upon experiences that have resulted in emotional responses. Each time an emotional response is chosen, the stronger the perception will become.

You have lived many lives, are a part of your lineage, and are in the present life you are in. All are contributing to your view of (or your response to) what you are experiencing.

The universe receives you by your perceptions, which it receives in the form of your emotions. The problem here is that often emotional responses are unconscious—you have no idea you are emoting as you are creating. And as you continue to hold a focus you have no awareness of, you will begin to feel you are being victimized.

In order for you to create from conscious awareness, you must start to be aware of the perceptions you hold that create negativity and choose to alter those perceptions to ones that create *positivity*.

An unconscious perception is a view you adopt based upon your reactions to your experiences. A conscious perception is a view you choose based upon the observation of those experiences. So in essence, one is the experiencer, and one is the witness of the experiencer. When one becomes a witness of their perceptions, they have the ability to adjust them in order to serve themself. So they use the human to feel and the source to observe and then choose their response.

This is mastery; it uses unconscious *and* conscious perception. The human feels, smells, tastes, and touches, and that data is used to draw conclusions, form perceptions, and establish beliefs. The higher self observes all of this and knows the choice they will make in how they will feel and creates the reality they will experience.

The master is consciousness aware of itself. As the master is aware, it lifts the human out of its unconsciousness and relieves its suffering by choosing to love. Once you have the understanding that you are not only the human and that there is a high energy source available to you, you can create consciously.

Creation occurs when the human experiences. Mastery occurs when the human has that awareness and chooses to align to it by living in joy.

How Do You Perceive?

Every one of you is a piece of the whole, the universe, all that is, or what some call God. All are the same—all are contributing and equally valuable.

By how you choose to perceive yourself in the world, each one of you has taken on a unique expression. The universe is responding to how *you choose*.

Many of you decide there are random things occurring over which you have no control. We would say stop trying to control those things (or anything, for that matter), and determine how you are going to use your free will to decide how you respond to attempts to control.

You are not here in fairness. You are not here free of contrast. You are not here to control the free will of others.

You are here in your sovereignty.

The Perception of What Is

Some of you choose to remain lodged in the perception of what is.

The senses you have are in place primarily so that you, as an experiencer, will come to a conclusion. If you didn't have strong emotions and feelings, if you didn't have your five senses to confirm your reality, you would not have the ability to expand all that is. You get stuck in your perception because you become your human experience. The part of you that makes you feel stuck is the part of you that feels. You will never stop experiencing or feeling, but as you grow, you'll gain the awareness of your perception and notice when you begin to get stuck in an experience.

When are you going to perceive something that is yet to be and bring it to form?

This is the choice you have in your sovereignty. You can agree with the masses and live a life that doesn't belong to you, or you can create a world for yourself that *does*. To do this, you need to believe in yourself, know yourself, and *love* yourself.

This is the conviction one needs to create their own individual reality. It takes strength, knowing, and perseverance. Many will say, "I can't believe because what I'm looking at is preventing that."

To that, we say you are looking at a sign of what you believe. When you can finally grasp this and own the example of your life that is before you, you can become the master of your personal reality.

Many of you don't have a personal reality. You are so guided by the reality the world has projected you cannot see your own.

You have looked at the masses and adopted the opinions of others. You have adjusted yourself to suit others. You have no idea of the reality you want to display to the world. You have become nothing more than a pawn in the game of life—but you can be the king. If you want, you can be the master, the deliverer of magnificence and the contribution that is you. Or you can simply decide to go along with the masses and make the opinions they have drawn yours. When you choose this, you fill yourself with suppression.

In this state, nothing good comes from the universe, only suppressed energy. People become sick, bored, or depressed when they are suppressed. Humans suppress themselves because they are fearful and because they feel weak. They are not brave enough to hold their own view. Unless someone agrees with them, they feel uncomfortable, which, in turn, makes them fearful. They want to be loved, and they're willing to give up themselves in order to gain love. All humans do this to some degree.

We often see this in couples. While we are not saying there shouldn't be compromises, we are saying there should be no hiding because hiding becomes suppression. "I have to suppress because the things I'm hiding are not in alignment with the one I'm with." But suppression is suppression. Either get into alignment with the one you want to be in alignment with, or get out because you will never be able to manifest from a place of suppression. You are giving up on your own universe.

You give up your own universe when you make a clear decision to not live in your truth, meaning you behave in ways that are not in alignment to you. You need to examine your close relationships, specifically how you portray yourself in them, and decide whether it is in alignment with the truth of who you are. Feel where you are uncomfortable and where you are not in your truth. "I'm going along because I'm afraid that if I don't, I won't be in alignment with these people."

This is the way that one thinks they're pretending, but pretending isn't really pretending because the universe perceives the real you. If you decide to not be in alignment with yourself, then you're cutting off the intricate connection with the universe. When you're portraying yourself to others in a way you think will be acceptable, all you're doing is wasting your time and causing yourself damage. You aren't living in reality because reality is who you really are and who the universe receives. Pretending is a fruitless endeavor.

Why would you choose this? Why be with a group of people or a spouse who makes you feel you have to hide who you are? You may think your mask is firmly on, but the universe sees right through it. It knows your every thought, feeling, and deed. So you have to decide if it's more important to pretend and hurt yourself or live in your truth and strengthen your connection with all that is.

In addition, you're not even fooling the ones you are with. What will happen is that those you are in relationships with will perceive you in not truth, not trust, and not honor, and *you* have to deal with this false reflection of yourself. You begin to believe you aren't trustworthy and honorable because you are the giver of this perception.

For instance, say you are in a relationship and you are not in truth. There are things you are hiding and lying about. You may say the relationship you are in is the cause of your hiding and lying, but in truth *you* are the hider and the liar. As you stay in the relationships you use as your excuse for not being in truth, you are not getting your intended lesson. That relationship is mirroring back to you your own lack of confidence and self-love and your need for acceptance. Instead of choosing to become a hider and liar, why not become confident and empowered by who you are and let the relationships that are not in support of that end? If you hide and lie, there will be an endless stream of situations you will continue to encounter that will match the energy of hiding and lying. It doesn't matter how others are perceiving you. All that matters is that you are in truth. The source is perceiving the *real* you, not the you you are projecting or hiding. The high part of you can only connect with the human in its alignment to itself. So stop pretending to be something you are not for anyone else. It just doesn't work.

Perceptions are formed by your experiences in this life, past lives, and your lineage. Here is an example.

A mother, while pregnant, experiences an injustice. She is very angry. Many years later that child reaches adulthood and has a lot of pain in their body. When asked about what emotions they feel when they are in pain, they respond that they feel an injustice, that their situation is unfair, and that they are angry about the pain. They are unaware why they feel this way.

As they explore each pain area, the same emotions keep coming up over and over again. What is confirmed is that even in the womb, the child absorbed its mother's pain and carried it into the life it is living.

Conscious awareness of emotions can often assist someone in releasing them and resolve the associated pain. If the mother of the unborn child had awareness, she could also look back and realize the injustice she suffered was brought to her from her own lineage. It's not important to figure out where the emotions originated but to identify and consciously ask to transcend them. By this way of examination, one can observe how they feel when they have pain and identify the emotion attached to it. Once they identify the emotion, they can choose to heal it by simply asking their higher consciousness to assist them in healing. "When my back hurts," for example, "the emotions I feel are anger and injustice. I would like to release those emotions and therefore release the pain in my body."

Arguments happen when you try to force someone to agree with you. You will always feel negative as you do it. There must be a compromise made and a meeting place that allows for each to create from sovereignty. There is no right and wrong, so you will never feel good if you try to create it. That is your source letting you know you are moving away from alignment.

Any time you feel determined at all costs, you will have more things coming to you that you will need to fight for. There simply is no need to fight for anything. All you need to do is experience and choose what you prefer and direct your focus to it. Stop thinking you need to change others in order to get what you want. Just want it and get it.

After all, your universe is a compiler or an accumulator of energy. Anything you have ever put your focus on or energy into is in your universe. It's yours, and no one else can use or have it. And it doesn't matter if it's positive or negative energy. Maybe you don't get the first marriage that you love. Maybe you don't get the job you love, and maybe the first business you create doesn't take off. What you do get is all the energy you put into it. That's yours forever. As you go about your life, you start putting good stuff in your bags instead. Thanks to that first marriage, you know what you want in your relationship. You know what kind of job makes your heart sing. You have a different idea of the business that you want to be in. Now all of that energy comes back to you, and you get your success really fast, and you get a great relationship really fast. You may not know how it happened, but we do: it's because the energy is already in your universe waiting for you.

When you direct your focus at every experience, you benefit by knowing what you want because of it. Now you are the master. Nothing is a failure, and nothing is for nothing. Simply say, "Now I know what I want, period."

However, if you get focused on negativity and go back into the old bags, you might build more energy and experience some things you don't like because of it. Being a master is choosing to feel good or the higher choice even when the human isn't feeling great. "I must have had a big accumulation of something in me that I needed more energy built up in order to overcome it, so for now, I'm going to allow it. I'm not going to patronize myself for it because I know when I get myself aligned and feeling better, I can draw on this energy that I'm creating." Energy is energy; there's no good or bad to it, and no energy is ever wasted.

Sometimes, if you are stuck in the tool or the human, the only way out of it is to accept it's stuck. Then you can throw yourself a bone by saying, "I am creating more energy even though I am feeling negativity. This beats condemnation, which will only drive the tool deeper into regret and lower feelings." This is a tool you can use when you cannot reach mastery—you just have to love the human and not condemn it. Try soothing it with the conclusion, "Eventually I will feel better, and when I do, I will get credit for this energy I deposited through my suffering."

When one reaches a state of mastery, they can feel the negativity and immediately look for the lesson in the experience—not become it. They can be grateful for it and then move on. The master doesn't blame someone for the feeling they have, and they don't condemn the human for having it. They simply know they have created it and choose to create from there by deciding how they will feel about the experience.

Take off the blinders so you *can* see, run your *own* race, and keep your gaze forward.

Sometimes, however, you'll get stuck in an experience where you keep returning to the same producer of negativity. You find yourself in a continuation. Often humans who are on a spiritual path get frustrated by this. They think they should know better and be able to deny it or move on from it. Instead, we want you to change your perception.

What if you looked at what is happening as happening for your benefit? Maybe you need more contrast in order to build more energy because the pattern you have within you that is keeping you stuck is so large that you need to keep generating more energy through negativity to overcome the energy of your block. We often see this happen with lineage blocks that started with a mother or grandmother. It is often something you have no control over the creation of, so instead, you have to build more and more energy until it becomes so dominant and unignorable that you will burst through the pattern and unstick yourself.

Contrast is wonderful. It works for you. Isn't it good to know that you, as a human, have this kind of force working within you? You have no awareness of it as it does whatever it needs to do to overcome what needs to be overcome. So don't deny the negative experiences. Negativity is transformational energy. You may need to keep dipping your toe in contrast, feeling worse and worse and worse. But your toe isn't getting dipped for nothing—it's getting dipped because you need a big charge of energy to be able to move forward and overcome your block.

Determined to Be Determined

We are going to keep picking off reasons your manifestations are not reaching you. One of the biggest issues is your opinions.

The strong opinions you hold are often in opposition to someone else's opinions, and holding tightly to them takes you out of your alignment. It makes you vulnerable to getting stuck in your human. You have to realize that the opinions of others don't matter—and to some degree, yours don't matter either. They are just an accumulation of feelings and emotions that you are experiencing, which are based upon all the lives, lineages, and experiences that are deposited within you. These are the compelling factors in how you perceive now.

While perception can be changed through education, understanding, and knowledge, many humans choose to follow along with other people's perceptions like goats. They choose to blame their perceptions on their lineage, on their mothers and fathers, but the reality is that they have simply decided to agree with what was presented before them instead of deciding to form their own opinion.

Many do this with their parents. You can become like your parents and not even recognize that you are giving up your free will and your ability to choose your life in your sovereignty.

You get an idea, have a preference, or come to a conclusion, and then you *insist* everyone else join you. You decide you are right and they are wrong. You live this way, so *they* must live this way too.

You are determined to be determined. Why do you insist on insisting?

Once again, we find ourselves talking about sovereignty. In your desire to be right, to have your opinion be the opinion of everyone else and govern how others choose to perceive, you have invited the energy of dominance and control to rule you and your universe.

Why must you justify everything that supports you in this behavior? You are in violation of human law. There isn't a human on your planet who wants to be controlled. Free will is your right. It is their right. It is everyone's right.

When a human has an opinion about how someone else is living their life, it is usually because they have perceptions based upon how they were raised. These perceptions translate into telling others how they should do things.

This is denial energy, and when you move into it, the universe perceives denial, so it denies you of all that you are wanting. Your manifestations are dead in the water. You've given up everything that you've worked so hard (through contrast) to bring yourself because of your denial of another's sovereignty—and you don't even realize you're doing it.

The perception the universe responds to is the admission of an emotion. It doesn't care if the emotion is for someone else because that someone else is actually *you*. You are part of all that is, the mass that *everyone* comes from.

Let others have their own perceptions and their own opinions. Let them do what they do. The only reason you're in opposition is because *you're* in opposition. When you stop, these people will fall away from your experience. The only reason you attract people to you that you don't like is that you focus your emotions toward them and tell them what they can and cannot believe. If you insist on continuing to tell people what to do, the universe will continue to send people who, in your perception, need to be told what to do. In other words, you will be surrounded by people who aggravate you.

If you feel disgusted by another and the way they are living and you deny them, you're going to experience separation. This separation you feel as you deny another is an indicator that many humans miss or ignore. They feel justified by this icky feeling of judgment, even though it doesn't make them feel good.

Look at feminism, for instance. Initially, when women were trying to equal themselves to men, they wanted to believe that there were no differences between women and men. After a time, women realized that they didn't like that as much as they thought they would. They've come to realize that they don't want to be viewed as men are viewed because women are different. This is not a negative, just a fact.

As time has gone on, women have come into their power not by changing men but by changing themselves. By expecting equal pay, respectful treatment, and acceptance in all fields, everything began to change. Rather than hating men, they choose to love themselves and feel worthy.

The real key to everything is how you *feel* as you do it. Often when people want change, they hate the ones who won't change. This won't result in change—it will result in opposition and conflicts. Aligning to those who support change and who love women and respect women will result in change.

You're not justified in any feeling that doesn't feel good, because that feeling is the higher part of you communicating that you're separating. You want to pin this bad feeling on other humans, when in reality, the feeling is yours, based on the thoughts and actions you are taking. Your connection to the source is responding to that feeling.

When are you going to make the connection to how you feel as you do this?

You feel control; you feel dominating; you feel forceful. And in the end, you feel unsatisfied by the response you are receiving.

We have told you the universe is perceiving you. What could it possibly perceive when you insist on controlling others? A denying energy. So the universe will now deny you of all of the things you want to create in your life.

Every human wants to be an experiencer who draws conclusions and creates their own reality. What another decides doesn't have to be a part of *your* reality. Make your own in the creation that is you.

There is nothing more fulfilling, nothing more gratifying, than adding purposely to yourself what you wish to see in the world. So many of you have forgotten this powerful ability you have to create from your focus. Don't squander it on anything that you don't want to see in the world—be responsible, accountable, and focused on what you will add to all that is.

How do I feel? How do I feel? How do I feel?

The perception you have adopted and focus on can either have a positive or negative effect on you. If it's a negative effect, you'll know because you won't feel good as you focus on or push your perception on others. You perceive the world first through your senses. But you also perceive through the eyes of those who are important to you, those who raised you, and those in your lineage who have passed on. A lot of lineage is passed through your energy centers. There are patterns of thought and emotion that are lodged in human bodies that get transferred into the little bodies that are coming in. As a creator, you can choose to operate from the bags of your lineage on autopilot, which is what many of you are doing, or you can decide that you are the maker and filler of a brand-new bag. Put something in your bags that you would be proud to leave to your lineage instead of continuing to use the bags that were left to you.

You have a choice to stay with the perceptions that you have and not question them at all, or you can make them fresh and new and decide that you want to feel good about your contribution to your future lineage.

Remember to ask for assistance—you are never alone and always supported, but you need to *perceive* a universe that exists to assist you. The universe *wants* to assist you; it wants to *support* you. And it *will* serve you.

The universe delivers through its connection to you, and you determine the level of that connection through your belief in it. Every single thing depends upon belief because belief is what supports manifestation (and everything you want is tied to that concept).

You are the one who creates, knows, and trusts. This is the gas in the tank—it's what runs the car. Fill your tank with belief, otherwise you're just running on fumes.

You won't get very far on fumes.

Oppositional versus Denial Energy

Oppositional energy is when you are trying to convert another to your way of thinking, while denial energy enforces, controls, or pushes your opinion on others.

Occasionally, oppositional energy will interact with perception and how we perceive. There will be things that you are opposed to that you are exposed to that will cause you to have oppositional energy, where you feel right in yourself. If others will line up behind you in the rightness of what you think, you believe it supports your ego and the idea that you are worth following because you are the "right one." In essence, you are looking for confirmation bias. You are shoring up your belief in you.

Are You in Love with the Universe?

There's nothing more attractive to the universe than you being in love with it.

Remember the yellow sweatshirt story from Chapter Three? The universe wants you to feel the magic, fun, surprise, originality, and intricacy of it. The universe loves to replicate positivity back to those it is interacting with.

There is nothing in this world that is working against you. Many humans think the world is a place to be afraid of or watch out for because it's going to hurt or be cruel to you. That is a false belief. Take that out of your bag right now. The universe is an all-encompassing, all-loving, all-knowing, and all-providing source that is answering all the calls that you, in your experiences, are delivering to it. We can't understand how that could be something not to love.

Think of it this way. If you had a partner who loved you, praised you, supported you, answered you, listened to you, and aligned with you, would you love them? Of course you would. Guess what: you already have this partner in your universe. It doesn't need to be lied to, doesn't need to be made to accept you, and doesn't need you to be or act a certain way. It doesn't care what you've done or how you've lived your life. It loves you always, forever.

How can you love the universe? When you love everything you lay your eyes on.

We keep telling you the universe is you and it is responding *to* you. How can you think you can be in this love-hate relationship with yourself and your surroundings and get the results you want?

The master—a human who becomes the source, who has connected to such a degree that they have a steady flow of source—begins to get the realization of what they are, who they are, and how they create. They create through their ability to choose to love and feel good. They can also choose to use contrast to their benefit rather than their demise.

The master doesn't believe in victimization and luck; they believe in creation and skill. They have found their key, the pot of gold at the end of the rainbow, the treasure chest. What was unknown has now become known. Frustration has been replaced by realization. What isn't there to love about that?

How could the master ever have believed they were powerless, that somehow they entered an existence over which they would have no control?

One must first know what it is like to be a servant before they can ever become a master. One must feel the opposite in order to manifest the counterpart because in opposites, something wells up within that could be created no other way.

Some humans would call oppositional energy negativity because it doesn't always feel good. But, as we've discussed, with this oppositional energy, you are building energy because you are in conflict with something. You aren't letting the energy flow through because there's something lodged inside of you. Another human could have the same experience that you're having an aversion to and, when they experience it, the energy flows right through them without effect.

When this energy gets stuck in a human, it's because they're opposing it: "I don't like it. It's not right." And they continue to generate more of what they are against. Instead, know that there is no reason to oppose anything. You are never going to change the way a sovereign being views the world or what they are in agreement with. You can't force them, even if you chain them up. Think of your prison system. You are never going to harass anyone out of anything. They'll continue to express as they have chosen to express, and the more you try to change them, the more you are going to create opposition within yourself.

Many of you humans will try to justify yourself as you read this. "Well, this human did this thing, and I cannot possibly agree with that thing." That would make you innocent in that situation, as if you were not a vibrational match to that person you disagree with. We are never going to agree to that. We're telling you right now that you already didn't like the thing that person did, or you would not have attracted them to yourself.

You need to be neutral. Now, we're not saying that you have to accept it or that it has to be a part of your experience, but having a heavy feeling about it or heavy emotion about it is to attract more of it. You need to get to the point where you can see someone do something that you do not like and decide, "This person is the way that they are. That is their expression of themselves, and I'm going to allow them to have it." Then gently move away because it's not something you want in your experience. Don't move away in denial or change. Move in neutrality. You can decide it's not of your choosing but don't have hate, distaste, or dislike of the one who is doing it. Remember they are a sovereign being and creator, and there is a match out there for that person. Focus on what you love and want to be around instead.

All experiences are exactly what are needed in order to fuel the creation that is unique to you. Adopt this love of the universe, and know it serves you in every emotion you experience. Gather up your appreciation. Allow and believe in the complete perfection that is unfolding before you. It's molding you and forming you because it *is* you.

Perception Is the Creation That Is You

Doesn't it make you smile to know that all you need to do is live and feel and then live the way you want to feel?

Why must you make that so difficult?

Have you ever heard it more clearly and simply than that?

Why do you live and feel and decide to *not* live in a way you want to feel?

It makes no sense to us at all. We keep giving you the keys, and you all keep changing your locks. Why do you continue to lock yourself out of your own house?

Because you don't own it. Anyone or anything can walk in and out of your house, and you do nothing to protect it. You give away your keys to everyone else and let *them* own *you*. Then, you use them as your excuse for the resonance you offer (or don't). Live how you want to feel. It's that simple.

There has never been a more important day than the one before you. Begin each day as though you are born again because when you chose to be born, you were an experiencer that couldn't wait to begin experiencing.

You have two eyes, two ears, a nose, and a mouth, and these were given to you so you could sense your environment and choose your preferences.

What will you choose to look at?

What will you choose to listen to?

What will you choose to breathe in?

What words will you speak?

How will you use your senses to perceive your environment?

Perception is everything in the creation that is you. The way you look at something and feel about it is your perception. How you choose to focus with these senses you are given is how you will manifest upon the earth.

While you won't be able to have 100 percent of any one perception you hold, the dominant perception that you hold as you view someone or something will be the contributor to the experiences that you are in.

Emotions are no mistake—they are the essential tools that form your perceptions. You see, you hear, you smell, you speak, and the universe receives the energy of emotions that those senses provide and responds. These senses, and the emotions that come from them, are your direct link and connection to the source that fills your body and breathes life into it. Without emotion, without senses, you would be nothing more than a blob of flesh incapable of knowing yourself.

We have told you that emotions, your sensing of them, and what you call negativity at times, is never going away. We have also told you that living consciously is critical to receive what you choose to believe. You are feeling and sensing and then *choosing* what you want to create by the choices you make.

How could you ever do it by denying emotion?

If you did this, there would be no choice to make. Many of you are of the belief that a negative thought is a failure—it is only a failure if you decide to hold it. Train yourself to be the feeler, the thinker, the *master*, the one who feels all but holds only what they wish to call to themselves. Feel yourself; feel your preference, and be the star in the movie that is you.

We would love for you to make fun of this—be more humorous, more accepting, and more knowing of how you create. You have to feel the contrast to do it, so why judge yourself and others as they are on their journeys?

When you feel the bullwhip, or what we call the contrast, rather than *be* it (or be upset by it), *use* it.

What do we mean by *use* it?

Know the feeling you just had holds a message for you. If someone leaves you out and you are hurt by it, know that through them, you are being shown a vulnerability within you. Whatever grabs your focus and will not let go of it is the wounded part of you crying to be heard.

Many of you humans think you must pick a wound clean, like the bones of a fresh kill. This isn't necessary—you can simply decide to leave the remains behind and move on. You may be surprised, especially since many of you have the practice of reliving and regurgitating everything you experience. This is what we call justification energy—all it does is justify a reason to feel pain. Choose your joy. Choose the way you would like to feel, and then send the messenger on their way.

Sovereignty knows that it is individually choosing, deciding, and proceeding on anything. When humans start to watch the news or listen to their group of friends, they start to perceive and believe what they are saying. For example, say Robin had a group of friends who were all single women who didn't like men, and all of them complained all of the time about men. As she hung out with these women, she would be flooding herself with their perception, and soon, her perception of her relationship could start to change—and that might change the outcome of her relationship.

What we mean is that the influence that people, ads, groups, friends, etc. have over us is our unconscious attention to how we feel while we are with someone, watching something, or in a group. Obviously, Robin probably wouldn't normally feel good if she was in a group bashing men. But if she was a little unconscious of herself and her feelings—for instance, if she had just had an argument or event occur that attracted those men-bashing women into her life—she might, in that emotive state, join them in it. It is crucial to take notice not only of the influence of this in your life but of the emotional state you are in that has attracted it to you.

When you have a perception about something, you choose things that support it. The perceptions of the people you're around are an indicator of your perceptions, and if you don't realize this, you may add something to your bag that you don't want. Make a decision to be aware of yourself, and remember that the ones surrounding you are going to support the belief you want to have in your universe. Many of you will think that you are being influenced by outside forces, when, in fact, the outside forces are nothing more than your own creation of what you're offering.

Back to our example. The women who hate men are there for one reason and one reason only: somehow they match something Robin is emitting. She could be one who stands up for men and therefore has opposition to those who criticize men. She may have gotten in a dispute with her husband before meeting these women. Or she perceives men negatively herself. The universe responds to your responses and matches them. Your job is to pay attention to how you feel, notice if you attract a situation or people to yourself that is not to your liking, and instead adjust yourself to what you are liking. That's what reality is: it's a perception you hold that is reflected back to you to view so you can adjust how you want it to be.

Chapter 6

DO YOU HAVE TO BELIEVE IN ORDER TO RECEIVE?

RIGHT NOW, AS YOU LIVE the life you are living, you are choosing how you feel about the experiences you are having. Based upon those choices, you are forming future incarnations that will live out the reflection of those choices.

Many of you will reexperience things repeatedly and not get the lessons you created for yourself in prior lifetimes. Don't worry; you'll get another chance.

Throughout this book we discuss mastery, what it is, and how it can serve you. Mastery is your ability to transmute negative experiences into positive learning growth. It's what you call free will. You have a choice, an ability to decide if you will be victimized or empowered by what you experience throughout your life. We hope you choose your universe and create a life for yourself that sets you up, both in this life and in future lives, for

higher-consciousness living. When you choose to feel appreciation, gratitude, joy, and love in spite of all you are feeling, now
you are equal to your source and a match to it. Once you are able
to obtain this level of mastery, you will live a life of joy. You will
understand that you have created the experiences you are experiencing, enabling you to free yourself from them and emanate as
source in human form.

You are living in a reflective universe—there are reflections
coming from various origins:

1. You have your lineage, which has primarily formed your
   beliefs.

2. You have your blueprint (or a plan) of things you want to
   accomplish or transcend.

3. Finally, you have the view you hold of yourself in the life
   you are in.

You are all that is experiencing itself through your human
form—and all other humans are doing the same. You are reflect-
ing back at each other (by matching each other through attrac-
tion) how you feel and what you believe about yourselves. As
you push against someone (say you disagree with their political
beliefs), you start to experience yourself as an opposition energy.

All interactions you have with another human show you
what you are projecting. They may reflect something you don't
like very much. However, it's *you* who is projecting that energy—
and you may have been for a very long time without being aware
of it. *What you perceive is how you're received.*

In your closest relationships is where you will primarily see your view of yourself. If you are stubborn, often you will have a mate who will reflect that back to you. You will find yourself irritated by a view you receive from another that you don't *want* to see in yourself.

Say you're in a relationship with a lazy partner, and when you leave them, you say, "I'm never going to be with one of those again." Yet a few months later, you find yourself with another lazy partner. That's because you didn't address the root cause, which is with *you*. Maybe there's a part of yourself from childhood who had to do everything yourself and could never count on anyone to help. Maybe you never felt *worthy* of help. It doesn't matter where it has come from. It matters that you are staying in your judgment of that person, and the universe cannot separate them from you. To the universe, you are the one emanating laziness, so it's bringing you lazy people. It believes that you focus on what you like, so it brings you more of your focus. The universe isn't trying to persecute you or aggravate you. It's bringing you what you are calling for.

Whatever the reason, you are focused on something that is consistently bringing lazy partners back to you. And until you address it, you'll continue to attract the same type of partner.

The way to address it is to recognize what is born of it. You want a helpful, engaged partner, so now knowing this, because you've had that experience, you can simply adjust your focus to that. "I want a helpful partner." You don't need to spend a lot of time figuring out the origin of what you have manifested that you don't like—simply identify what is liked and focus there.

When you address it, you can drop the bags of your own self-perception and enhance your life.

What is enhancement? Enhancement is, quite simply, anything that makes you feel good. It's an awareness of when you are in connection and when you are moving away from connection. Said another way, enhancement is a description of expansion. It's making all that is better, bigger, and boosting. In all your experiences, this is what *you* are doing. You are expanding yourself by experiencing and forming your preferences. Remember, you are the creator in human form.

We Are Fans of Knowing

We want to enhance your life.

We have come in support of you, in the belief of you, in honoring you, and in the feeling of you. Your success is our success, and the energy we feel as you expand is always unique and credited to *you*.

Go ahead and play the pinball game. Keep launching those balls with the intent of hitting a big mark and gathering all the points you can. Keep trying, and you'll get better and better and better. Enjoy it. Play it with others, and see how high your score can go. Feel how *good* it feels as you score and rise as a player. And every time you finish the game, come back again and again and again to achieve the highest level you can.

- How have you played the game so far?

- Was it with intention, skill, experience, and belief?

- Or did you just show up and pull the handle, release the ball, and *hope* for the best?

We're not big fans of hope. We're fans of *knowing*, but knowing gets created through intention and dedication. Hope implies there's something random happening (luck) and a last-ditch effort for the powerless and the non-believer. We've heard many humans say, "I can hope," and we say, "We hope not." Hoping isn't assured. Hoping is desperation, waiting with your hands out for something that may possibly be satisfying. Hope is not belief.

We want you to understand there's nothing wrong with aspiring for grandeur. There's nothing wrong with wanting to *become*—what's wrong is wanting to be something for someone else. Don't hope to become something. Don't hope to be accepted, admired, or held in high regard. Instead, know that you came here with a vision for yourself. "This is my contribution, my enhancement, and my expansion. This is why I'm here."

We want you to understand that you need to follow *your* guidance system. Don't allow another person, in your fear, to govern you to do something that isn't suited to you or your life path. Hold a vision of success, and with this type of conviction, there is nothing you can't achieve.

Your Ability to Know

Go ahead: entertain yourself, and read all the books you can about self-help. Take the long road to a destination that's in your backyard.

You already have everything you need to solve the problem you have. When you are connected to all that is and all that you are, everything becomes available to you.

Many of the things you read in your self-help books (when you are not connected to your source) will cause you to condemn yourself. You will begin to notice all the things you're doing wrong and end up on a roller coaster ride that is detrimental to you. If you feel as if you can never aspire to be whatever is being projected in these books, stop judging yourself, and start loving yourself for noticing there are things that you would like to transform. Look at your study as a tool that will open you up to the wisdom and knowledge that is already within you. Don't look at it with your amnesia and condemn yourself for not remembering; give yourself time to remember.

There's no special way to practice anything. There may be certain practices that feel good to you and align with you energetically. If it feels good, you'll increase your chances of manifesting what you want, so you can use it to your advantage. However, you don't have to rely on that practice to get what you want. What you're doing is agreeing that when you do this practice, you're going to get specifically what you want from it.

Yet we often see humans become frustrated because they don't get what they want, even though they're practicing repeatedly—because ultimately, your transformation will come from your source and your belief in it.

The real power of anything comes from the source of the power, which is belief. If you pour yourself into an object and give it to someone, telling them, "I have poured all of my energy into this," and they grab it and say, "I'm so grateful to have this with your energy," and they truly believe it, their energy will align with it. If your energy aligns with a tool, it can provide value to you. This applies to any type of tool, such as tarot cards or pendulums.

Many religions are offended by these objects, and we don't understand why. It's the same divinity that they speak out in their churches coming through the tool that they have asked it to come through. When you use tarot cards, you have an intention and a desire, and divinity rolls through the cards, as you believe it will. Belief in the source activates the source. Belief in a divination tool activates the tool—this is true of all practices as well. Because you are the source, and as you believe it, then it is so.

They are simply a vessel for energy.

If you aren't in alignment with one practice, try another. You may have to search.

You have an unbelievable amount of power and ingenuity available to you. But for some reason, you humans have been made to believe you don't. You have become limited in your 3D reality, so stuck in your physical form that you're blocking out the multitude of realms that surround you. You simply need to open yourself up to them as you opened yourself up to this one.

All of the wisdom, knowledge, and understanding you are searching to receive is already in you. This is a book from you *to you*. You aren't learning from the words you are reading—you are learning from the desire you have to know. But you have to believe in your ability to know, or you will forever seek it through the knowing of others.

This is not to say that you cannot dabble in the paths of others or try out the many practices that exist. Perhaps they might ignite something that stimulates your belief and works for you. But the process of unfolding you have to do on your own. It is the journey you are here for. You cannot take the journey of someone else and make it your own.

Easy to Be Negative

Many humans get very upset when they're experiencing negativity in their lives. However, even though you've come to this plane as pure, positive energy from a vibratory level of love, you are coming into a very dense, negative plane that requires a lot of you to exist upon it.

When your pure positive energy meets the dense negative plane, you'll experience contrast (the bullwhip). You're never going to be able to totally avoid the crack of the whip. It isn't wrong that you're experiencing it, but you have to decide: do you want to stay in negativity, or do you want to obtain mastery of yourself and choose how you feel about an experience rather than just reacting to it? When you stay in negative experiences and react negatively to them, you create separation, and your desires move further away from you.

You'll think you are feeling increasingly negative because you don't have what you want. But it's really because you don't have a chance at getting what you want because you're losing your connection to the one that's funding you with it: yourself.

You are connected to the source, to all that is, in every moment; it is guiding you and wants you to stay with it. If you start to bicker with someone, realize that you have separated from yourself (i.e., the source). Because you are the creator, the one you are bickering with is *you*. The exchange you are having is simply evidence of the negative thought you created prior to your exchange. We want to laugh at you as you tell us about conflicts because in our view, conflicts don't exist. We know that all beings are sovereign and have the free will to choose. As you try to force, coerce, control, and dominate, you'll feel terrible—as you should. Why? Because you will never take away another's sovereignty. You can only use your own focus to produce what you want to produce.

So why be upset about the argument?

Who should you be mad at?

Yourself—because you attracted the argument in the first place.

When you understand this concept, you can start to understand that how you move is reflected back at you.

"The checkout lady is really crabby with me."

"The cab drove right past me."

"What am I emanating that I haven't been paying attention to that's being reflected back at me?"

Every human has their doubts—the voice in their head that whispers their fears. But the human who has the doubts and hears the whispers and keeps going anyway is on their way to becoming a master.

A master isn't *without* doubt—they are *with* perseverance. They cannot stop; they cannot give up. The universe knows this person believes because if they didn't, they would not continue. They'd hit a bit of a struggle and drop the ball. In this way, they'd never achieve or receive what they want.

In contrast, the master keeps going until they catch their creation. The master knows it's already there the second they desire it—all they need to do is align and become a match to it. Once they do this, their doubts fade, and the whispers disappear. They become confident, knowing, and powerful in their ability to create.

Once you persevere, life becomes a responsive, cooperating, and collaborating game that you play over and over and over again. It's okay to have some doubts and worries along the way as long as you keep believing, push them aside, and keep going anyway.

Loop Thinking

If you find yourself stuck in a loop or pattern of thinking, what should you do? Clearly you don't feel good. Why do you stay? What's there for you?

We'll tell you what's there: the justification from yourself that you're not the louse you think you are. You are stuck in defense of yourself.

The negative feeling you have is notification from the high part of yourself who is in disagreement with the view you hold of yourself. Change the view and watch how quickly you bounce back.

"I am respected. I am worthy. I know my own value."

BAM! You'll be right out of your loop.

Many humans believe they are stuck in a loop unjustly. However, whenever you have to start justifying your behavior, that is your first signal you are entering a loop. There is no reason, ever, for you to have to justify who you are or *what* you are to anyone else. Justifying signals you are in a loop of not believing or being clear about what you are revealing of yourself to others. If you are in your authenticity, there won't be a loop because you don't have to justify who you are.

What You Believe You Receive

Let's talk about what is holding you back from your goals, desires, and fulfillment.

It's quite simple, really—there is only one thing that prevents you from your fulfillment and that would be you. How could it be you? It is you because somewhere, someplace, you have decided to deny yourself what you in your sovereignty want.

Based upon your observations of others, you have decided what you will and will not allow yourself to have. As you perceive your universe, you begin to *believe* in it, and this is how you will receive it.

Perhaps you have viewed some things you unknowingly focused upon and deposited in your universe. Maybe you never even noticed, never really had control of it; maybe you were unconscious of it.

If your mother was a stay-at-home mother, that created your perception of what a mother should be. So even though you're a mother who loves to work, you're going to stay home and be miserable because that's what your perception told you to do.

Instead, create and honor your *own* self, not in the view of what someone has placed before you. There are many who want something, but they're afraid to allow themselves to have it because someone in their life deemed it "wrong." You have to know yourself, decide for yourself what you truly want, and then get that. Remove everyone else from the equation.

If you don't live this way, you'll be denied on the other end because you're denying yourself. The result of that denial is how you are perceived. Denying yourself will lead to a mediocre existence. After a while, you don't really know who you are because you've denied it for so long. You have not lived in your truth. You have no idea of who you really are because you've conformed yourself to all those you've been in the presence of.

We have said in past transmissions there are many things contributing to your perceptions. There is your lineage, and then there is the many lives you have lived. You may not know your lineage, but you don't *need* to know it. All you need to know is what you're struggling with.

What is a recurring theme?

What is something that is repeating in your life?

It could be within you because it is an inherited perception or belief that has been passed down to you. (Then you go on to form your own perceptions and beliefs, add those to the ones you've inherited, and send the whole package down to your own children and their children.)

You have to become self-aware of what you love and are choosing. Get to know yourself on a deep level so you are a depositor of self-love and self-knowing rather than a depositor of what you have perceived in someone else in your life.

Sometimes a human will knowingly make a modification in themselves. They want to liken themselves in a form or a way that would serve them better. If you are in a way of thinking or believing, and it's detrimental to self, yet it *is* who you are, sometimes you will willingly view someone else and modify your behavior. This is different from just being a follower because you are doing it by choice. You are making a decision for yourself. Perhaps you've seen something in another that you find admirable, and you want to add it to yourself. This is not denying the self; it's bettering the self.

Whatever you have viewed, especially as a child, becomes very quickly adopted into your universe. You call it inheritance. We call it unconsciousness creating.

Now you are armed with the new awareness of being mindful of what you choose to focus on. It is way easier to build up resistance than it is to remove it. If you came from poverty, if you viewed lack, it is deeply rooted within you. Stop watering the weeds. Stop allowing them to spread, and start to slowly choke them out by thickening the green grass. Keep reminding yourself that no one determines the outcome of your life but you. You do not kill weeds by denying they are there; you kill weeds by understanding how they grow. Be gentle with yourselves. Be patient. Be understanding. Soothe yourself when you notice things that you don't want in your garden. You do not need to look for weeds and pull out every single one. All you need to do is redirect your focus to the thick green grass, and it will do the work for you. In other words, focus on a new way, and create a new garden.

Anywhere you are denying yourself you are preventing your creations from coming to fruition. You must pluck out the beliefs of others that you have adopted that are limiting you. Don't blame them. It is you who has agreed to what you have viewed. Move forward, and see the world through your own eyes and not the eyes of others.

You hear a lot of talk about resistance. What is it really? It is anything that denies you what you are wanting based upon what you have agreed to in your view of the masses. You are not here to deny yourself anything. Don't let anyone shame you, guilt you, discourage you, or determine how you create for any reason. Have your preference, and honor it. Create the world for yourself independent of what you have viewed, but rather, create by how you feel. How do you want to feel? How do you want to live? How do you want to express yourself? Let go of your upbringing.

Let go of your masses, and experience yourself as sovereign and free. No matter how you were parented, no matter how you have lived in your past, you are an individual expression of source. Cut the cords, and once and for all see yourself as you really are, a god in human form.

Reflective Universe

In your work, you may struggle with finances, or you may struggle from having wealth. Both are reflections of beliefs and comparisons. It does not matter which struggle you have; the lesson is the same. You are here to discover your power to create the experiences you are choosing. There's no need to be poor and no need to be guilty if you are rich. You are the creator of the experiences you are having. The recognition of this is the goal.

In your life you have a culmination of encounters everywhere you go. This is what you humans would call luck or bad luck. A pleasant encounter at the store: good luck. An unpleasant encounter driving to town: bad luck. This is the area you really have the most control over because you are not so emotionally connected in these encounters. These are quite simply an overall projection of your emanation to the universe.

A good analogy is when you tell someone, "You're acting like a child." They don't want to hear it. What you could do is accept it. Tell yourself, "I'm acting like a child." And then consider why. Now you can consciously, as an adult, know why you behaved like a child, and your subconscious mind will no longer control your instinctive reactions to situations. The more you do this, the more you heal past wounds and reintegrate aspects of yourself into yourself. This is part of becoming whole. The recognition of what you are receiving, mirrored to you in your interactions with others and life, is exactly how the universe is perceiving you based on what you have emitted to it in your emotional responses.

We would love for you to be more attentive to this because this is really how you view your universe or perceive it. This is where your most control is. You do completely have control over the everyday annoyances that you are reacting to. Where you put your focus on in the masses and where you individually choose will show up in your daily experiences—this is where you can play or begin to manipulate form. Prove to yourself how your focus can actually influence your everyday life experiences.

We love the idea of gratitude, appreciation, and praise as a means to manipulate form. It removes your personal feelings about yourself and allows you to generate good feelings based on what others are receiving. In this way, you are now attractive to the universe whether or not you personally feel that way. This helps you achieve the results you want that maybe you've not been able to get or feel for yourself.

It's that simple: be genuine, and create a positive view of yourself by those you are viewing in love.

Chapter 7

ARE YOU CONSCIOUSLY LIVING?

WE HAVE MANY CLIENTS from many different cultures and belief systems, and that includes those who love their churches. We would never contend that any of it is not worthy of worship or not true. What we will contend, however, is that it is your dedication and love of it that makes it so. You are never not the creator. You are never not creating, and forever, wherever your focus is, there your belief will be also. Where your belief is is where your reality is.

We're often asked if tools such as psychedelics or crystals are things humans can use to achieve what they want to achieve. We are never going to tell a human they can't do something that they want to do and that makes them feel good as they do it. After all, that's part of your human experiences. Do you *need* to do it, however? No. But do you believe in it sometimes? Yes. And if you believe in something enough, it can help. Not because the tool did anything but because your desire for it to work is making it work.

You are using the tool to create, but the tool creates nothing—you do. If you're drawn to a practice and it makes you feel good, it can yield you something you want, but never believe that using tools is a necessity for you to achieve true connection with self.

True connection with self is the love of self, the understanding that you're not wrong, you're never going to do anything wrong, you're nothing to be ashamed of, there's nothing bad about you. Once you can really sink your teeth into this understanding, how could you ever judge yourself again? How could you think that you are less than or worse than anyone else for any reason? You are an experiencer, and the way that you perceive your experiences is not based solely upon the life you are currently living—it's based upon your previous lives, what your ancestors have left, and now by how you are choosing to perceive the life you are living. How you control that is based upon the understanding that you need not become the result of your experiences, but rather, you can choose the result you want out of the experience you had.

If you follow the masses—say you read about a study and the supporting ideas on what is healthy or unhealthy for you—be sure that you pay attention to how you are choosing to agree with it. Are you afraid that if you don't follow, you will not be healthy? Or are you choosing it because it feels good to you and will, in turn, be good for you? To some degree, when you look to the masses, you give your sovereignty to them. Whether or not that is wrong would depend on how you are perceiving: in fear or in your power.

The False Idea of Enlightenment

You have to learn to stop judging yourself and simply allow yourself to have experiences. Don't blame other people for how you feel. The feeling is yours. It's not shameful or wrong. Your human is simply experiencing, and you should never judge it right, wrong, or otherwise. You only need to allow. That's all you're here to do.

So many humans want to be enlightened. In our opinion, enlightenment is darkness. What you are doing when you become "enlightened" is shutting off your emotions. You decide to be a stiff, perfect, flawless idea of perfection that someone has brainwashed you into thinking that you *should* become. This is false.

Humans believe that to be enlightened is to become something better than or higher than what they are. They have the perception that the being that achieves enlightenment has achieved something very difficult only available to the lucky few. They have the idea that a really spiritual person would never swear or raise their voice. All of these are false beliefs. Mastery is achieved by a human mastering awareness of how they feel and then choosing how they prefer to feel. It is pure awareness of your source and your alignment or misalignment to it.

The Universe That Is You

Every thought, emotion, and *word* has a vibration and energy. It is through this vibrational energy that the universe is sensing, feeling, and *knowing* you. The energy you send out is your signal, and the universe receives that signal and responds to it. The vibrations you emit are how the universe perceives you.

It's a language that many of you have no awareness of. As you emit your vibration that comes from the life experiences you have, you (in all that is) expand immediately. To experience expansion here in your physical form, you need to hold a level of frequency that matches you in all that is until it makes its way to you.

The resonance of all that is, is the highest level of love. That is how all your experiences are received. You match that by appreciating the experience, gaining the lesson from it, and choosing to feel good because of it. You can't match it in negativity.

This means that when you launch a desire to all that is, that desire leaves you at a specific vibratory level. To manifest that desire, you need to stay at, or get back to, that same level. The faster you can get back to it, the quicker it will come back to you. Re-create, as close as you can, the longing and emotion you felt when the desire was launched. You can even put a number or code to that feeling, the way you would detect the rate of an earthquake. Some resonances can be felt across the board, such as the satisfied feeling after sex. The emitting of satisfaction sends a level of vibration that calls for you to be satisfied, which is why it resonates to many areas of your life.

Imagine being a universe all by yourself. As you live your life from your perspective, you have desires for what you'd like to experience. You're doing it at every moment, whether you are aware of it or not. These signals are released into your individual universe. Once they are there, they become part of your universe. If you hold the signal (or feeling) long enough from the desire you had, it will work like a homing device calling it to you.

Unfortunately, you are constantly so affected by the contrast, you have a hard time holding yourself in that feeling long enough to receive what has been created by it. Notice we said what has been created *by your feeling*. The universe is returning something that will match the feelings of the desires you have had. Everything is out there circling you, looking for a way in.

If you are mostly *positive*, you will draw things to yourself that in your human form will feel pretty good. (Though, as we have said, we don't agree with the labels good and bad. We agree to expansion, which we get no matter what you experience.)

But let's say you've had a lot of *negative* experiences. You've looked out into the masses and used them as a means to determine why your life is as it is, and now you've invited a very large mass of negativity to circle you. All you need to do is have a few down days, and the signals you put out may line up with negative experiences, drawing them to you.

You're not necessarily getting more positive experiences by adding them; you are getting them by *matching* them. The more access you will have to the things is dependent on your focus, either positive or negative.

The universe is receiving every experience you've had, but you can't receive it in form unless you become a match to what you have sent out. It's like a radio station: on a clear night, you can find it very easily, but on a night where there are a lot of clouds, you may get a crappy station with a lot of static. And on a stormy night, you can't tune in at all.

One of the best ways to draw to yourself what you have been wanting is to stop wanting it. Why is this? Because this signals the universe that you know it has been created: you believe it, and you're not questioning it. There is so much resistance created in wondering where something is—in impatience waiting for it, in the lack of trust in it—that it simply can't make its way to you. You just aren't a match in that energy.

Many of you will become discouraged when you don't receive the thing you want right away. Or you'll get some things you are wanting, but there are some recurring experiences you don't like that keep coming back around. We would tell you this is a very clear example of the resonance you are holding. If you were honest, you would admit that the thing you don't like keeps recurring because you have maintained focus upon it.

Sometimes you are holding a resonance from childhood. Parents can have a great influence over their children because the children love them and believe them—their parents are in a dominant position. And often, children are too young to do anything but receive the perception their parents are putting on them, so they start to believe it.

"He's a naughty boy. He's a troublemaker."

The child gets into more and more trouble because he believes in the perception of the parent. And because he believes in that view, the universe is going to yield to that view.

As adults, you have to learn what your view of self is.

Is it the view that everyone mirrors back to you?

Sometimes, some of what they mirror can belong to them; however, you can't forget that you are the one who is perceiving yourself as you are receiving from others. You need to consciously decide: *Do I believe that? Did that hurt me? Am I going to hold that as a truth for me?*

What you consciously choose to believe is what the universe

will yield to you because that belief becomes the vibratory signal you are sending.

This is why you need to be sovereign and send your *own* signal into the universe. You don't have to send the signal of every person you come in front of. Start every day with the intention to live consciously. You'll be amazed at what will transform in your life.

We make this point to depict to you why your relationships can seem wonderful one moment and awful the next. It's because you never hold the view or feeling of when it is wonderful long enough for what you want to manifest. You keep justifying your negative emotions and responses, all the while filling your universe with probabilities for things to come to you that you don't want whenever you lower your vibration.

Think about it: you have your own personal universe, and then there is the mass universe or consciousness. What you perceive and believe is your contribution to your own personal universe, and it then becomes a part of mass consciousness, or all that is. You are picking and pulling things from your universe based on how you *feel*. Yet some of you add to your personal universe the thoughts, feelings, and perceptions of the masses. Now these, too, are part of your universe and become accessible to you.

We know you can't help it: you have two eyes, a nose, and ears. But if you arm yourself with the wisdom we are offering, you can begin to pick more carefully, not just from your senses but from your understanding: *What I perceive matters. What I believe matters, and this is how I will receive.* Only add things you love to feel from mass consciousness. Be indifferent to everything else.

What Is Consciousness?

What is consciousness?

It is your source. It is awareness of itself.

You humans are often aware of nothing other than the tool you are experiencing life with. Consciousness knows it is creation; it understands its power through its awareness and focus.

Consciousness is all that is. It's every experience and *the* experience.

A human is an ever-evolving, ever-expanding piece of all that is. Even right now, as you read these words, you are having emotions, feelings, thoughts, likes, and dislikes, and these are creating your future for your current and future lifetimes. Think about it. Does it make sense that you would live this life for nothing and then die, go back to the source, and ask another being, "Would you like to be my husband in the next life? Would you like to be my sister in the next life?"

Or would it make more sense that through all of your exchanges and emotive value for the experiences you've had, you are creating a passageway into the next lifetime you will live? You are the creator, and that never stops because *you* never stop. It's not like you're here today, gone tomorrow. You're creating your tomorrow right now. It doesn't even stop when you go to sleep. Why do you think some children are born into the world music ready, computer ready, art ready? They were born with this based on what they created for themselves in previous lifetimes. Your now moments matter because they are your tomorrow and your future. Your past doesn't matter. It's yesterday's news—unless you are republishing it today and going to run that copy again.

Consciousness is the wisdom of all that has ever been. It is everything that has ever been done; it has reunited with itself and knows itself as this. As consciousness enters the earth, it projects itself into the human tool to remember that it is the wisdom, source, and culmination of everything and everybody.

The source will always guide you in a direction that feels good, and it will also notify you when you're headed off course with negative feelings. You keep thinking something has caused you to feel negative, when in reality you've chosen to go against yourself. *That* is the reason for negativity.

Conscious living requires you to know the difference. The experiences mean nothing! It is your reaction, your *decision*, that means everything.

"But someone cut in front of me!"

"But someone blamed me!"

"But someone did something to cause me to be upset!"

Conscious livers are aware *all the time* of *all the events* and *all the feelings* they are presented with. They know they are the ones who draw their experiences to themselves based upon how conscious they have been. If you had not chosen to go against yourself, there would be no one against you.

Somehow, some way, you have to make this important observation and shift.

Everything that comes before me has been created by me.

Why would you ever blame anyone or anything ever again?

Every human is on a journey toward alignment with themselves.

Once you grasp this all-important, all-encompassing concept, you will no longer be in conflict with anyone about anything. When you focus upon someone who is not to your liking, you are inviting what you are not liking. Gain the wisdom to know that all negative expressions are consciousness that is not aware of itself. Every human is struggling with this understanding. It's why they project how they feel onto others and use them as the excuse to be unconscious or in negativity. Have compassion, understanding, and love for your fellow man and know that he, like you, has done nothing more than focus his consciousness without awareness on something unwanted. How could you condemn him for that?

The Difference between the Conscious and Unconscious

Do you know the difference between a conscious and unconscious person?

One is aware, and the other is *un*aware.

How many of you live your day-to-day experiences but have no awareness of how you are using those experiences to create emotions, which in turn create your life? If you are not aware of this, then you are unconscious—you are unaware of what you are doing in every moment of every day. You have an experience, but you are unaware of the importance of how you are feeling it, so you react based on that unawareness. You choose it, so you unconsciously create.

You are choosing to be the human. You're judging yourself, stuck in the hate, anger, jealousy—whatever the emotion is—and you have no idea what you're creating. As you succumb to these emotions, you feel that it is reality and get stuck in the body that you are in. Once you can understand that you are not the human, you can understand that you're not expected to judge yourself or do everything perfectly. When you are consciously creating, you are not stuck, and therefore, you don't have the same responses or reactions that you have when you're being the human.

What if you became aware that you have been given opportunities through life experiences, and you have to choose how you want to feel in the life you create?

This is consciousness aware of itself, and this is what you intended to do here: create consciously through your awareness. You have an experience. You are aware of how you are feeling it and react based on that awareness. You choose your reaction, so you consciously create.

Create Consciously

We have stated if you know anything, know this: you create. And we're going to keep on saying it over and over again until you realize there is no one or nothing that you haven't summoned to yourself.

Start to form new ways of attracting what you *want* by the revelation of receiving what you *don't want*. Use these unfortunate moments to create more fortunate ones. Don't penalize yourself for something created that is unwanted—simply notice and determine what you prefer and refocus.

You are going to create one of two ways: consciously or unconsciously.

Why make something complicated that is quite simple?

Consciously choose how you would like to feel in any given situation you are in. Otherwise, you become your emotions because when you get the emotion, you are fooled by it. You start to think, *This is me. This is my life. I am poor. I am not good looking.* You decide, because of the emotion, that you are the *emotion*. But you are *not* the human tool. Your tool is just having experiences, but when you become the emotion, your higher self cannot reach you. You need to choose how you're going to feel rather than staying in the negative feeling that created the experience.

The emotion is coming from your higher self and is an indicator of your connection or disconnection. As you become the human, you are disconnecting from your higher self. You begin thinking negatively of yourself, in judgment, shame, guilt, loneliness, depression, etc. That's when you feel the emotions: sadness, anger, frustration, fear. These emotions are a sign of separation from your source. They are how your higher self tells you that you're not going to manifest the things you want unless you start moving your back over to them.

When you find yourself all worked up and in an emotional state, know that you have unconsciously chosen it. Knowing this is how to become conscious of your creative power.

As a human you will never *not* be emotional, as to be emotional is to have a preference. You can't avoid it, but through your unconscious creations, you can begin to modify how you choose to get the life you prefer. Simply look at an unwanted thing or feeling, and decide from that place what is preferred.

When a negative experience happens, you can choose how you feel about it and decide what you want to feel instead. You can also pre-pave good intentions for yourself. Before you go to an event: "I want nice encounters with people." Before you drive anywhere: "I love drives that are peaceful and relaxing." And when you have these good experiences that you pre-pave with your intentions, show plenty of appreciation for them because that will be the creative value that you receive back. Put more focus on your positive encounters than your negative encounters, and you'll receive more positive encounters. Focus on the negative, get more negative.

This is a big "aha" moment for you. There are so many of you who squander your power—you go through your lives as though you are trying to pin a tail on a donkey with a blindfold on. This is how unaware you are of what you are emoting. You simply become the emotion and use it to justify your actions rather than committing actions that justify an emotion. It's backward, in our opinion.

You call it right and wrong, but we would prefer you say what you would like to receive. You prefer to justify who is wrong and use that justification as a means to create more negativity.

Is that right? If creation is based upon feeling—and it is— we would never justify anything that didn't feel good. We would drop anything that was headed in the opposite direction of where we wanted to go.

Be a seeker of truth, humility, trust, honor, and everything that feels *good*—and don't worry about those who choose something else.

Create a fortress around yourself that no one can penetrate. Decide to rule your own kingdom. Don't open your drawbridge to every conflict that comes before you. Keep it closed. Turn away, and let them take their wars someplace else.

Focus on Your Full Buckets to Fill Low Buckets

When a human sees their bank account get low or fat on their body when they want to be thin, it can be very difficult to pull your focus from it and onto what you want to see. In these situations, go to an opposite area in your life that you feel good about. Leave the low bank account behind, and instead, focus on your great relationship with your spouse or the love you have for your child or a favorite hobby that brings you joy.

As you focus on the area that you are already feeling great about, that "bucket" will overflow with positive energy, and that overflow will seep into the low bucket without you having to focus on it.

Your Life, Your Choice!

If you are an unaware emotive being, you attract negative experiences to yourself. Often, the result of what is occurring is what you are reacting to; you have no idea what you have done prior that has caused this result.

You are the creator of your upset. There are no victims, only creators.

So make moves to enhance your feelings, experience, and power. When you see something you don't want in your experience, consciously reframe what you see to how you want to see it. We know *you* know that you can't get where you want to go from where you are.

Think about this: if you stand in the same spot but wish to be someplace else, you're not actually going anywhere. You must *move* from the place you are to where you would like to be. Sometimes this means consciously choosing a different path than the one you are on.

We think that many of you walk through mud and slop rather than the nice smooth, dry path that is available to you. Why do you continue to choose the difficult response to everything when there is another much easier, good-feeling choice available to you?

You humans all talk about living a simpler, better life. What in your mind is a simpler life or a better life? It is a life you are choosing as opposed to a life you have unconsciously imposed upon yourself.

"This is the life I *have* to live; I have a mortgage and car payment."

You reinforce upon yourself what you *don't* want to do and rationalize it. However, anyone can liquidate what they have today and be gone tomorrow, if they so choose. But many won't. You are prisoners in your fear—prisoners in the lives you're living that you don't want to live. You are imposing this life on yourself.

So why do you have to always believe that somehow, someway, you have been made to do something you'd prefer not to be doing? All that occurs when you make a change is your choosing. Choose the lives that suit you, make you happy, and bring you into alignment so you can create in your unique expression, through your alignment to your authentic self.

If you were to analyze yourself and the way you create, you would very quickly gain a very deep understanding of many of the scenarios you have in your life. Things go well: you feel good, and so you choose things to support the belief that you are worthy. Things don't go well: you look out at the world and choose things to support the belief you have that everyone is struggling and having a hard time.

This is how you create unconsciously and how easy it is to get sucked into the masses and give away your sovereignty. When you do that, you feel like you don't have to accept the responsibility for the life you've created by how you've chosen to perceive, believe, and receive. You're just a victim, right? Wrong.

We want you to understand that you are the one who creates, so how could you be a victim?

You decide what you choose to believe. Don't be afraid of a negative thought or experience. Simply know it's part of contrast so you can choose, and then choose mindfully. *How do I want to feel?* It's really that easy.

What do you want to create? How do you want to feel? Choose it.

Repeat over and over to yourself, "Know one thing: I create." And remember that this is *never* not the case.

You are a creator. If you don't like the life you're living, create a new one by focusing on what you want.

Chapter 8

IS AUTHENTICITY IMPORTANT?

AUTHENTICITY IS WHAT YOU KNOW about yourself. It's your thoughts and feelings. You know who you are. You can pretend to be nice when you're not or pretend something doesn't bother you when it does, but you and the universe will always know the truth.

We have talked to you about authenticity and the importance of being authentic. This is a driving force in manifestation that is often overlooked. This type of realization and acceptance is what we call alignment, or another term: understanding.

Hiding provides you with nothing. You are hiding from yourselves when you present a false self.

How will the universe ever find you in hiding?

How will it recognize you?

The universe has a view of you that is you. You know who you are, and so does the universe. When you lie to yourself and others by being someone you are not, you can't connect to your desires because they belong to the authentic, not manufactured self.

The universe rewards alignment, truth, and understanding. It rewards the belief, "I am worthy just as I am." Authenticity invites everyone and everything to come into alignment with you.

When you are in your authenticity, everyone you draw to you is going to be authentic as well. People who are in their authenticity are connected: they will have opportunities for you that would not have otherwise revealed themselves. When you are in your authenticity, you are in alignment—you are sovereign, powerful, and a creator. Authenticity puts you in the driver's seat and gives you the opportunity to co-create with other sovereign, authentic people.

Opportunity comes through connection. It comes from those who *know* they are the creator of their own experience, not from those who play the victim. When you can move into a powerful, connective state where you don't care what anyone else thinks of your authentic self, you enter into sovereignty.

We aren't saying you have to be difficult to be around, but if you are difficult, you must *own* it. Don't hide from it. Don't pretend to be something you are not to make people like you more. You can't create the life you want by becoming a character for someone else.

Enhance and Expand Your Life

You humans have to try to prevent everything, and again, it's because of your belief in definitive right and wrong. How do you possibly consider the studies you have done that cannot possibly take into account all that has transpired in each one of you, in regard to health and wellness?

I am sure you agree that your ancestors play not only a great role in your inheritance of your health but also in your happiness. How can you know that a study applies to you? How can you know if you are one of the ones who has aligned to this way of being?

You do your tests on how to eat, how to exercise, how to not eat, how to have less stress, how to not smoke, how to not drink, etc. You will fight with all you have to confirm the result of your studies that are done. However, you have no way of knowing how the universe is perceiving the one who is being perceived. If they are in alignment, if they truly love their life and themselves, that is not possible to study. Why? Because they have no problems. There would be nothing to study: they would be happy, healthy, and thriving with the life they want.

What if someone loves the greens, loves the healthy choices, loves the exercises? What if their ancestors were the same? No one considers how much happiness this could possibly be bringing to the ones who love it.

What if someone loves something else? What if they love to eat fatty foods, drink, smoke, etc.?

But because of what the masses say, they deprive and restrict themselves because of what they have deemed their "wrongdoings."

Did you ever once stop and think that what the masses think influences the masses? So much of health comes down to your perception of it—it comes down to your *belief* in it. Believe what you can do, and it will be. We are not claiming that science has no basis, but we would say your agreement to it is the biggest basis of all. Think about the people who live to one hundred. Do you think they ate healthy every single day of their lives? No. Some of them smoked cigarettes and ate whatever they wanted.

Scientists who study long life spans don't do an analysis of people's happiness. For instance, people who drink a few drinks a day could be very happy and not stressed at all, but do scientists consider this? No, because they are trying to find people for the studies who are in compliance with what they are trying to perpetuate to the masses. The scientist's job is to prove their theory correct.

What we are trying to communicate to you is that it doesn't matter when you choose to leave this plane. You as an individual creator cannot determine for another what their creation will be. Whether or not you deem certain behaviors to be life-shortening, each individual, based upon their ancestors and their own feelings and thoughts, will determine their individual outcome.

If you choose to live a life you deem is unhealthy based upon the views of your masses, then of course you will be unhealthy. This is the reason for poor health. You may argue that science states that certain behaviors are life-shortening for a large portion of your population, but we would argue that all of you have the right to choose and to live in a way that makes you feel the most alive.

Any human who inhibits another human from living a life of joy will most likely not live a life of joy themselves. Let each other choose the life they wish to live. Let them eat. Let them be merry, and let them enjoy all the things that are available and align to them. Stop deciding for them how long they are going to live because of your choices.

We know that many of you controlling humans will not agree. You will say you just want them to live longer, healthier, more productive lives. We would say live the life you wish to live, and allow others to live theirs.

Some humans feel as though they are not living the lives they want to live because they limit themselves in the pleasures they enjoy. Some would rather live in a way that adds years to a life that belongs to the masses and not themselves.

Do you not wish for our fellow man to be sovereign and to choose to explore and to live and die the way he chooses to?

Or do you want to choose how he should live, how long, and how you tell him to do it?

This is ridiculous.

Why do you need to extend someone's life rather than focus on enhancing your own?

How Do You Feel?

Many of you do not pay attention to how you feel. You simply *react* to how you feel, but you never identify *why* you have the feeling. You think it is about the one in front of you, so you blame them, blame the situation, and blame everything except yourself.

If you feel disrespected, change.

If you feel unloved, change.

If you feel worthless, change.

The emotions you feel are nothing more than the emanation of yourself in response to your beliefs by what you have agreed to adopt into your universe.

So many people don't like things about themselves. They get

angry fast. They talk back. They do X, Y, or Z. They have attributes about themselves that they want to change.

Unfortunately, as you focus on what is not liked or wanted within yourself, it only gets stronger. There is never a time when you are not drawing more to yourself that you are focused upon—and that includes your need to be perfect. Perfection comes in love, acceptance, and honoring of self, not in judgment of who you have deemed yourself to be. Love and accept yourself as the experiencer you are, and your source will transform you in all the ways you are wanting.

While you do need to be able to get along with others to some extent, you still have to honor yourself and these traits. You have to allow yourself to express yourself in your unique way. Some people may move away from you, but there are many people who will gravitate *toward* you—and these are the people you'll want to connect with.

You don't have to connect with everyone. You're looking for the right people for you.

Many humans play a character, and in doing so, they're not authentic. They are projecting a version of themselves outward so they can be perceived in a way that is accepted. But the universe knows you. It can feel you.

You may fool other humans, but you're never going to fool the universe. It's why people will say they don't understand why an experience happened to Joe down the street because the perception that Joe gave them does not line up with what the universe knows about Joe. This is the first sign that you are not authentic. Joe may even believe what he's putting out there. With enough effort, people can actually fool themselves into believing they're something they're not, but that doesn't mean the universe is going to believe it.

Create Balance within You

Every aspect or emotion within you has its opposite. Don't deny either—both are authentically part of you. We want you to feel your life, and we want you to recognize all of your emotions as your own. Notice the imbalances.

In order to live a balanced life, you must look at *all* authentic aspects within you and balance them. Remember, the universe perceives you by the feelings you emit to it.

When you become out of balance, areas of your life become separate or a problem. For instance, if you're a workaholic, your relationships may begin to suffer. Be sure to have an awareness of all of your areas—work life, relationships, community, etc.— where you funnel most of your energy, and where you could possibly be out of balance. This will be different for everyone.

If you find you are out of balance and you are struggling to get back into balance, especially with your manifestations, use the buckets trick discussed in the previous chapter. Soothe and acknowledge yourself, "I have two wonderful kids," and you can slowly soothe your human tool out of this space where it cannot come into alignment. Don't try to hoodwink yourself into believing something you know isn't, but instead, gently move your focus away and onto the good things in your life instead. When you do this, you'll immediately start to feel better: more hopeful, relieved, and relaxed. If you can hold onto this vibratory level, more thoughts, ideas, and circumstances will provide you with even more feelings of ease. Before you know it, that money will start to come, or the ideal man you want will show up. It's about finding a place where you can align and then allowing the other things to ride that energy wave to you.

The universe wants honor, justice, and balance. Create this balance in you, and the universe will respond in ways that will honor you. Neither turn your back on your fellow man nor give yourself over to him. Know the difference between the two.

Selfishness versus Selflessness

There is no right and wrong. Let's look at selfishness and selflessness.

When one is considered selfish, they are often not willing to contribute to their tribe or their group in equal ways. They will take for themselves rather than sharing equally among all. When one is considered selfless, they are more than willing to contribute to their tribe or their group in unequal ways. They will give more of themselves rather than taking an equal share among them all.

Each of these two aspects has its creative value, or its cause-and-effect response from the universe.

As you keep more for yourself in your selfishness, the universe simply responds by putting you into situations and circumstances where you will experience trying to get more for yourself. In essence, it will affect your flow or your ability to manifest freely. You will forever be striving to get something, but you will never experience getting what you really want because you have deprived others of what they want from you. In other words, the universe will in turn be selfish to you.

When you live selflessly, the universe responds by matching you to those who are selfish. You have convinced yourselves that giving selflessly is what a good human does, so the universe will put you in situations where you give, give, give. Selfless giving means exactly what it says: you value yourself less.

The selfish will feel guilt and shame, and the selfless will feel disrespected and used.

These are two opposites that when out of balance, neither is of benefit to each other. Both aspects are needed, and both are valuable, but it is important they work together in balance. There will be times that one must be selfish and other times that one must be selfless, but to be just one or just the other will not serve you.

Do you believe you should receive and not give?

Do you believe you should give and not receive?

Either way you are doomed. You should give *and* you should receive. The two are the same.

If you look into the lives of those who are selfish and those who are selfless, you will find that both the selfish and the selfless never have enough.

Why is this so? You are meant to have abundance. You are meant to receive, and you are meant to give. But in order for the universe to provide, it must be in balance.

You're not getting away with anything in your selfish behavior, but at same time you are not getting anything for your selfless behavior either. We are trying to get you to understand that what you deem as the right and wrong way to be is of no consequence to the universe. It simply denies those who deny themselves, and it hoards from those who hoard for themselves.

Be free with your love, help, kindness, abundance, efforts, and yourself, and the ability to receive in turn.

We are concerned with freedom and sovereignty to explore what you came here to explore—we are concerned with your authenticity.

You may not want to hear this, but if you consider your emotions, you'll realize you don't feel good as you argue against others. In every human lies the truth, understanding, and knowing, and when they are faced with each, they cannot deny them.

Authentic Expansion

Every life is an exploration, a journey in personal growth and expansion. No one ever said, "Stay as long as you possibly can, and deprive yourself of everything that the masses determine as not good for you." Quite the opposite. Life is individual, and no matter how many studies you do, you will never determine what is right for every sovereign being. All you are doing is deciding for yourself and then imposing that on everyone else.

You will go through seasons in your life, and you will very naturally choose what is needed to authentically align yourself to the life you wish to create. All of it causes expansion, learning, and growth.

You could never become great without becoming less. As you explore yourself in contrast—in poor eating, in poor exercise, in poor behavior, in less of what the masses deem as right—you actually become the opposite. But you will never see this result of who you have become as you continue to view yourself as less.

Expansion occurs in the contrast. This is the missing link that none of you can accept. We are not arguing that you are either right or wrong in any of your studies or observations. What we are arguing is that without those who do the opposite, the others can never reach a positive result.

When you choose to follow the masses, you essentially stunt expansion from reaching its potential.

No one knows the signal that is you except you and the universe. For anyone else to predict your health, outcomes, probabilities, and possibilities is impossible. How someone eats, acts, or conducts themselves is between them and the universe. They may be very happy with something you are very unhappy with. Happiness overrides all emotions. When one is happy, one is in alignment. Never override someone else's happiness by trying to convince them to be like you.

You may think you know how others are perceiving, but you do not. We have told you that the universe will deliver to you based upon how *you* are perceiving it. If you continually make it your business to project your perception of how someone else is living onto them, you will inadvertently project that onto yourself. In your rightness—by believing you know better than another—you have become the very thing you do not like.

To be happy is to be healthy. To be healthy is to be in alignment, and to be in alignment is to be allowed to perceive as a sovereign being. Know that the minute you start to perceive for another, you have forfeited your sovereignty and are creating based upon the negative view of them you have projected onto yourself.

When you live in your truth, when you live the life you came here to have, this is your alignment.

Live a life of experiences. Live a life of joy. Live a life of picking and choosing to feel good—and let others do the same.

Chapter 9

DO YOU APPRECIATE AND ADMIRE TO GAIN SATISFACTION?

ADMIRATION IS TO LOOK AT something or someone and be as happy for them to have it as you would be if you had it yourself. Appreciation is the understanding of how someone obtained what they have. There's an appreciation for the journey and the point that they have reached, while admiration is the recognition of one reaching that point. Satisfaction is the completion of both of those things: appreciation for the journey and admiration for the result. The combination of these two things is satisfying.

Our favorite example of this is two lovers in bed. They embark on this journey in the bedroom (appreciation) and experience their climax (admiration), and in the end, there is satisfaction.

Appreciation and Admiration Creates Satisfaction

We have advised you before, and we are again, to follow the breadcrumbs that are leading you to what you want in your life. Appreciation is gratitude to yourself for recognizing this journey you are choosing—and you are choosing it, whether you know it or not. As you go along and start to see the results of the efforts you've made in the direction you are going, admiration of self comes in. Look back at yourself, at all you've done on the journey, all the paths you've walked and leads you've followed, and admire yourself for it. Be thankful to yourself, and have admiration of self for taking that journey.

As you admire yourself in this way, there comes a satisfied feeling for the results that you've obtained and the climax you've reached. Whatever you wanted to get out of the experience you were experiencing, you've reached it, and now you feel satisfaction.

It's: I do this. I start to see and feel this, and then I have this. It's the wheel of creation.

Appreciate yourself in the way that you are following the path. Admire it as your manifestation(s) starts to show up to you, and then feel satisfaction as you complete the journey. Then, begin again on a new endeavor. This is the way we want you to live. You're never completely satisfied forever. If this was the case, you'd have one orgasm and be done forever. No, you're going to go back for more and more of that good feeling.

First and Last Days

Appreciation and gratitude are so valuable to you during your experience because they remind you to feel and to not miss out on the middle days of your life. When you forget to appreciate and have gratitude, then your experiences are unconscious, unnoticed, and unproductive. Use your time wisely. Use your experiences to dwell upon wonderfully so that you may be gifted more experiences that give you those types of feelings.

A day not recognized, not appreciated, not grateful for is a day you have wasted. When you waste things, it deprives you and others of things that could enhance their lives. As you live consciously appreciating and being grateful, not only will you have more of these types of experiences yourself, but your fellow man will as well.

Gratitude is where emotion is intentionally launched. Most of the time you are living unintentionally. In appreciation and gratitude, you're knowingly attracting situations and circumstances to yourself that are going to feel good. When you lack gratitude and appreciation, you deprive yourself of the opportunity for more—and you deprive everyone around you of more. You have a responsibility to be more, not just for yourself but for everyone you come into contact with.

There is nothing that you do that is not affecting the whole. All of it has an effect, cause, and result. You are the providers of love if you so choose to use your power, and you are the *deprivers* of love if you do not.

All you need to do is recognize your experiences and emanate emotions. Be grateful no matter what they are. Know that you, in your attention, are creating. You don't have to be perfect, and you don't have to always be positive. You just need to feel and choose what you would prefer to see in form.

Admiration and Sovereignty

Admiration is the revelation that everything is you. You adore another because he is there in your likeness. Somehow, some way, you have loved yourself in a way that has delivered something lovable into your view.

You viewed something in an admirable way, and it brought your vibration to the same level. Now more admirable things will enter your universe because of it. Admiration has a multiplication factor: the more you admire, the more you gain admirable things, so the more you admire, etc.

You may not always be able to admire yourself because you have not reached the point you think you should have or achieved the thing you wanted, but you can still emit the energy of admiration through your focus on someone who has achieved what they are wanting. Admiring another is a sneaky way to raise your vibration when you can't admire yourself because the universe doesn't know whether you're doing it to another person or yourself. It just answers that vibration with more things for you to admire.

Once again you give away your power. You look at the thing or the one you admire as separate from yourself and take no credit for its manifestation. We have told you nothing and no one appears before you that you have not summoned. Yet you continue to only notice the negative experiences and are all too willing to claim those as you.

We would love for you to admire more because there are so many options in that emotion for the universe to fulfill you with. You don't have to only admire yourself. If you're not experiencing everything you want to experience in your life, you can put your focus upon someone who has achieved or gotten what you want. This is a great place for you to start so long as you don't do it in a self-deprivational way ("they have something and I lack it") but in an understanding that "if I'm viewing it, it's available to me too." As you admire another, you should feel joyful and proud—feel as though it is you with that thing because it is you. Anyone in the universe can achieve anything because you are all part of the same flow of energy. Admiring another can be an assistive tool to help you get what you want.

It is an emotion that encompasses so many things, from relationships to money to occupations—essentially everything that is available in physical form. If you made a practice of admiration, you would add to your universe or orbit so many fulfilling things to connect to (just by staying in it) that you would be astounded. You are adding in every moment to your universe—why not intentionally add those things you love to see? Why not magnify, multiply, and increase your manifestations?

When you go to the grocery store to pick out fresh fruit and vegetables, would you not want to pick the container full of produce that is perfectly ripe and juicy? Or would you buy the container that is half rotten? Of course not. You are going to pick the best food to eat. In the same way, you should pick the best thoughts and feelings to have.

We wish you would look at yourself as the picker and chooser you are. We wish you would become pickier and choosier. It matters, it matters, it matters. What will it take to make you believe that? Look at your life, the reflection you are seeing, and know you have chosen it in this way.

Don't lay in the mud and expect not to get dirty. If you want to stay clean, you must watch what you step in. Not in judgment, but in common sense. Know that you are watching where you are going. If you piss and moan about your divorce, you are going to attract a bunch of pissers and moaners around you, and you're all going to be in the mud together.

Fans of Appreciation and Gratitude

Let us tell you why we are such fans of appreciation and gratitude. When you start to manufacture feelings, you are consciously creating. No one intentionally, consciously creates negativity, but there are those who intentionally, consciously create positivity. In essence, feelings and thoughts of gratitude and appreciation are you consciously choosing to feel good, and thoughts and feelings of negativity are you *un*consciously choosing to *not* feel good.

It is your natural state to consciously feel good. Your human counterpart's natural state is unconscious and, therefore, responds only to stimuli of life experiences as the determining factor of their happiness. The unconscious is the reactive storage house of pain, both mental and physical. So as you feel pain as your human, you become unconsciously stimulated, and the result is negativity.

The unconscious mind is the place where memories of pain are stored. When you are stimulated, either emotionally or painfully, then what is stored in your subconscious mind will activate, and an ungoverned response will happen—one that is not governed by your source but by your human. For example, take a person who was abused greatly as a child. If you were to walk up behind them and tap them on the back, they may immediately turn around and punch you without hesitation. Someone who was raised without abuse would not have the same response. This is because the abused person has had distrust, pain, and defense of self stored repeatedly in their subconscious mind, and when they perceive a threat, this response automatically comes forward with no thought.

With time and the right tools, you can make yourself consciously aware of what is in your subconscious. If you have unknowingly stored a painful emotion or reaction and then consciously recognize it, you move that reaction from the subconscious to the conscious mind. Now the reactive part of you won't be able to access it.

This is why humans have different reactions than others. One thing might be said to you that doesn't bother you at all, while another human may become irrationally irate. It's because all of the emotions that have been built up over many experiences have created a large ball of energy around this emotion, and so the reaction is equally large. Volatility in a human comes from repeat incidences that are stored over and over again in the subconscious and that cause the human to be responsive when activated.

If you find that you have an automatic response that is way bigger than the situation calls for, then it's a signal that you are touching on a large storage point in your subconscious, and you need to look into it. Ask yourself, "Where have I felt this before? When have I had this emotion before? Why is it so strong within me?" If you do this, you'll find a great list will start to form in your mind. You'll get flashbacks and memories from early in your life when you first felt this emotion, and you'll become aware of what is stored in this "file." As you become aware of each memory, you begin emptying the file because you're taking them out of your subconscious and moving them to your conscious mind. As you do this, you'll find you no longer have a large response, and over time, you can empty that file completely.

By choosing appreciation and gratitude, you can consciously manufacture positivity rather than allowing yourself to unconsciously fall prey to becoming the human tool. This is a decision that is made when a human decides that rather than being self-focused in every endeavor or encounter, that they are going to be more outwardly focused on others and what their experience is. As you look out at others and how they are enjoying themselves—how their day is going and how happy you are for them—you have removed yourself from the equation, and you will receive the benefit of your positive thinking. This is a great way to generate positivity if you aren't feeling good about yourself.

You are adding to your universe by the thoughts and feelings you are having based on the life you are living. This universe that is you belongs to you. You can choose what you want to feel more of in your life. Once you really understand that there's no upside to just allowing yourself to be victimized by your experiences and you begin to master your focus, now you can create exactly what you are wanting in your life.

Mastering your focus intends how it wants to feel, not how it feels in the moment. You decide how you view yourself.

The master manufactures feelings that they know will bring them the results they are looking for. They recognize feelings that are contrary to the result they want and simply release them and use them to their benefit as well. No thought or feeling escapes them, and this is why they are called the master. Every thought and feeling benefits them, so they have mastered themselves. You must learn to manipulate form by how you see it.

"I have a thought; I become more. I have a feeling; I become more. I choose the thought that best serves me. I feel the way it best serves me." Did we say you'd never have a negative thought or feeling? We did not. We said, "I choose, and therefore all feelings and thoughts are creative."

Do You Ever Ask Yourself Why Appreciation and Gratitude Feels So Good?

We'll tell you why: because anyone receiving it or giving it is rising in their vibratory level as a sign or signal of the alignment to itself. When you align to your source in your human tool, it will always feel good. Your source will always connect to you whenever you choose to consciously create, and conversely, it will disconnect from you whenever you choose to create unconsciously. Why do we say create unconsciously? Because source would never create unknowingly. Source would always be picking and choosing very carefully. Know that when you are stuck in your negativity, you are unconscious because when you are conscious, you know exactly what you are doing and why you are doing it.

Become the witness rather than a victim. Observe yourself in all of your feelings and thoughts. See them all for what they are:

choices. Be grateful, and appreciate all the choices you are presented with, for without contrast, expansion would be impossible. You could never conjure a better feeling, thought, or emotion without contrast. It is the vehicle for getting to where you want to go from where you are. You just keep getting better and better and better, and the longer you hold yourself apart from your expansion, the more negative your feelings and thoughts will become. They will grow to such a size and impact that you will have no choice but to succumb to them. All is well. All is perfect. You will meet yourself at some point; it is inevitable. This is the benefit of contrast. It will increase until you align to your source.

Contrast is the deliverer of what you want and don't want. It decides for you. You have to decide for yourself what you like more than what you don't like. Without contrast, you would have no way of forming opinions. You would be flatlined. We would much rather have you in negativity than in flatline because flatline produces nothing. At least with a charge of emotion, you have something to work with. You have a ball of energy being released to all that is, and you are expanding because of it. People who feel nothing don't expand.

Many people train themselves not to emote. They just…exist. They are so careful not to feel negative emotion that they no longer feel positive emotion either. They have come to the belief that staying in the middle is somehow safe. But they are simply fearful of creation because they don't know how it works. By becoming dead men walking, other humans aren't drawn to them. There's no offering, connecting point, or energy exchange, which is what you need to co-create with someone.

Some of you will decide to leave relationships. Some of you

will quit your jobs. Some will even end your lives, but none of you will ever escape the escrow you have created through contrast. The contrast will continue to present you with the same feeling experiences until you materialize your desires upon the earth. Pay attention to where there is intensity building in your life, and decide to figure out a way to align. Choose consciously what you really want when you are experiencing things you don't want: "I want more loving relationships. I want more harmony in my work. I want to live a free and passionate life." Know you have created it even in its opposite.

Admiration and Appreciation Create a State of Gratitude

When you feel admiration and appreciation, you create a state of gratitude. Now that you've created a state of gratitude, thoughts and feelings to support that state of being will be funneled to you through you.

Let's say this: judgment and condemnation create a state of self-hatred. Now that you've created a state of self-hatred, thoughts and feelings to support that state of being will be funneled to you through you.

How can you ever expect to be something other than what you are? When will you ever stop being surprised by the creation that is you by you?

We have made this as simple as we can possibly make it. You are the perceiver, and by how you perceive you will begin to believe, and now this will be what you receive. You have the ability through your focus to perceive in any way you would like to believe. Why do you continuously insist on perceiving in a way you don't feel good as you are doing it? Make a decision, "I'm going to perceive in one way, a way that creates, a way that is conscious, a way that feels good. I'm going to do it so fervently, so consistently, and so determinedly that I believe it with all my heart." Wait and see how the universe responds to that way of being.

Chapter 10

DO YOU LISTEN TO YOUR GUIDANCE SYSTEM?

EVERYBODY FARTS.

Imagine you are in close proximity to a group of people, and suddenly a foul smell engulfs the space. Is there any doubt that someone has passed gas? Everybody smells it. Everybody is disgusted by it, but nobody is willing to claim it. (Often, the people who have the biggest reaction to a fart are the ones who did it.) You just go on like it never happened and wait for the smell to pass. Something in you knows there is less embarrassment in the acknowledgment of it than there is in claiming it. Stop claiming your mistakes, shortcomings, and insecurities. Let them dissipate.

Acknowledgment is when you want to provide justification for it: "I ate a lot of cabbage and beans." Claiming it is claiming, "I farted. You're going to have to smell it." Claiming has nothing to do with the problem that created the gas. You become the gas without the acknowledgment of why you have the gas. Don't claim the cause of the farting; just recognize you don't like the smell, and move away from it.

There is not a single person in the room who hasn't passed gas, so there's no reason to be ashamed of it. We want you to feel and release, just like trapped gas. Some of you are going to find this analogy funny, but we can't think of a better example than this to depict holding onto things that are painful. Let go of anything that you do not feel good about. Love yourself as the experiencer you are, and know that while contrast is a part of life, attaching yourself to it is only going to create more of what you don't like the smell of.

You don't clear the air by admitting and becoming the bad smell. You clear the air by releasing it and letting it dissipate.

Your guidance system is knowing that if you supply others with truth and honesty, they'll forgive it. They'll feel your truth and resonate with it. Your guidance system will point you in the direction of authenticity. "I am not perfect. This is how I am."

What Is Your Guidance System?

When are you going to get that everything in your life is *about* you, *for* you, and *is* you? You continue to misunderstand your emotions, your guidance from all that is, as something other than what it is.

What is your guidance system? It is communication from you, to you, about you. It's your emotions. Every time you experience an emotion, it's your higher self communicating with you. It has nothing to do with the person or situation you are interacting with but everything to do with the stance or view you take about the situation before you.

Emotions are powerful because they're attention grabbers. Because humans are feelers, emotions get your attention very quickly. They cause a reaction in you that you're unable to ignore. Sometimes you deem this emotion painful or negative, something you don't want to feel, but all you need to do is reframe emotions as charges of energy. That's all they are: different forms of energy charges. The magnitude of the power of energy you feel in any given moment is how strongly you are going to react to it.

The master understands themselves and all that surrounds them. They don't blame themselves. They simply choose, feel, and liken themselves to what they like to feel. They don't determine whether what someone is doing is awful or bad or if they wouldn't do it that way. They don't care. They are simply searching for the things they want in their universe. Nothing more. They know they have the wisdom and consciousness to know and understand that anything they apply focus to is now part of their universe. The speed and magnitude of the manifestation they create will depend on the amount of time and energy they put into their focus.

You have a choice, and your emotions are the guidance of how you choose and what you will be likened to.

Did we say anything about good and bad, right and wrong? We did not.

Through your emotions, you will become the greater expansion of everything you experience in all that is. But in order to experience it in physical form, you need to choose your natural, higher vibratory rate in your human form. You have to align yourself to what you've created through the experiences you've had.

We know it can be a struggle, but struggle can be replaced with ease if you can understand that you create and you have the choice on how you choose to create. Anyone who has manifested anything in their life has intended it. Becoming a master is no different than getting your driver's license. You have to get behind the wheel and take the test to get your license. To become the master, you have to go through the process of first learning how to drive.

You also have to be gentle with yourself. When you first learn, you're all over the road. You take corners too widely. You drive too fast. The teacher will tell you to slow down and show you the best way to take the corners. Gradually, you will start to get a feel for the road.

This is how we want you to navigate the creation of becoming conscious of what you do in every moment of every day, as much as you can, so your life is exactly what you want it to be.

Be a Conscious Creator

It really comes down to being a conscious creator as opposed to being an *un*conscious creator. Both are creating. Both are contributing, and both are expansive. The conscious creator knows their value, knows their worth, and never judges themselves harshly. They experience contrast and understand they will emote, but they don't become their emotions. They follow their guidance system when they start to veer off course.

The unconscious creator doesn't realize their value—they feel unworthy and judge themselves harshly. When they do something they deem as unacceptable or shameful, they start to agree. They start to become what the people surrounding them are projecting at them. This is how you become human. They become the result of their experiences, attach to their emotions, and become result oriented. They rely upon the views of others as a means of evaluating themselves. If they're told that they're a naughty boy, they start to believe it. Then, they perceive that everyone sees them as the naughty boy, so now they fully believe it. Because of this belief, they become naughtier.

If only they knew that the view they agree to hold of themselves is the *only* view that can affect them. If they knew how to follow their guidance system, it would tell them whether they have chosen the view that would most benefit them. If the view they hold will serve them, they will feel positive, and if the view they hold *doesn't* serve them, they will feel negative.

Once you arm yourself with the knowledge there is nothing random in your life—you are deciding, picking, choosing, and agreeing to either the view another has of you or the view your source holds of you—you can begin to create simply by experiencing independent of judgment. You allow your emotions to reveal to you how you are being perceived by the universe by what (and who) is being drawn to you in your experience. No longer do you blame others, and no longer do you condemn yourself. You simply pick and choose in a way that gets you the desired result. The master delights in all that is revealed to them in their experiences and in everyone they meet because they know it is *them*.

Negative Emotions and Now Moments

Let's talk about negative emotions and your now moments.

A now moment is when you smell your morning coffee and feel refreshed or hear your lover's voice and think, *I'm happy to hear that*. When was the last time you smelled your coffee, took the first sip, and thought, *I'm really grateful for this?* It's noticing everything that's going on around you and how wonderful it is.

Humans don't understand how big these unnoticed moments are and how much they can produce for you if you would notice them. You have so many opportunities to love, feel, touch, smell, and taste—and you don't notice any of it. You might as well be tasteless, senseless, and blind! Feel everything. Feel your elimination in the morning. It's a good feeling that often goes unnoticed.

You do not understand your emotional guidance system. When you feel negative right now, *right now* you are agreeing to or thinking something the high part of you does not agree to. The separation you feel notifies you by pulling away and creating a negative feeling. In order to get your attention back onto something that will benefit you, try to observe, savor, and appreciate your present moments.

Say you're in an argument. You've attracted this to yourself somehow. And once you decide to engage in this behavior, whether you do it openly or hidden inside yourself, you'll experience a feeling of negativity. As soon as you identify it, be grateful for the experience and emotion of negativity you feel, and know that an opportunity has presented itself for you to now choose, in your mastery, how you will respond. Will you respond in the emotive state of your human experiencer? Or will you be grateful for the preference of what you really want that has been received in all that is and choose to align to it by simply loving the human for offering you the experience?

The universe knows the feeling you're having, whether you verbalize it or not. You can't hide from the universe. You may think because you aren't speaking your thoughts and feelings, you are getting away with something. But in your ignorance, you damage yourself much more than anyone else ever could.

Rather than trying to love someone you hate, focus on more love. Understand you can't use a negative to get a positive. You have to choose the positive. Stopping hating isn't the answer—don't even look at hating. Only look at love (or whatever feeling you desire) to get the results you want. The universe doesn't care about justification. You are simply sending out a signal for something you want or don't want. Know yourself because the universe knows you. Every feeling, thought, and deed is known.

Then you, being the human that you are, move to justification, or all the reasons you should feel negative and shore yourself up in your rightness.

"Here is the negative experience."

"Here is this awful person."

"There went my money."

"I don't feel good."

"I'm not sleeping well."

All the while, you unknowingly regenerate more and more separation, more and more negative emotion. Once and for all, you have to accept that nothing random is happening to you. You have to realize that somehow, somewhere, some*place*, you've allowed your guidance system to be ignored. You felt negative emotion but kept doing the things that caused it anyway.

Where have you been unconscious in how you feel in your life?

This is the question you must ask when you are experiencing *anything* you do not like.

Let go of how you got there and figuring it out—decide right now to drop the bags and feel *good*. Be accountable for the mess you find yourself in, and clean it up.

Any time you find yourself in a situation you don't like, take the other person out of it. Go right into yourself, and figure out what you are doing to attract this lesson to yourself.

Humans constantly tell us that they want to become more spiritual and connected. But you cannot get more connection than the emotional communication that you have with your higher self in every moment. Those emotions are your high self talking to you. Start listening to it.

Humans are always looking to feel good because the source that is the real you wants to feel joy, love, happiness, satisfaction, fulfillment. Then, when you feel negative emotion or contrast, you appreciate it for allowing you to see that you are moving *away* from what you want to become. Simply choose to use that signal to redirect. It's difficult to experience something that is so contrasting to yourself. It's like getting out of a warm bathtub and jumping into a pool full of ice. It's going to be shocking. It takes a conscious creator not to ignore the senses that are screaming, "This is cold," but to understand them and then embrace them for the creative value they can add instead of recoiling from them. Let them flow through you like a screen door.

Making Mistakes

Whether in tune with their guidance system or not, every human makes mistakes. It is not your place to point out others' mistakes. You don't even have to point at yourself for *your* mistakes; simply learn from them.

Always pay attention, when you're following your guidance system, that the activation within you is authentic. Is it coming from your guidance system, or is it coming from a wound, a place within yourself that you have not tended to?

Make *no* mistake: the situation would not be before you if you were not a match to it. This is where your accountability and responsibility come in.

The reason you don't want to take accountability or responsibility for being the creator you are is because then you'd have to admit you have been living unconsciously. That *you* brought something you don't like to yourself. It's much easier to blame it on the neighbor, bad husband, or whoever else you can find. This is the normal reaction most humans take. But you should love the ones who are punishing you because they are revealing a vulnerability in you that you need to learn from.

Why do you keep insisting it's about someone else? Everything appearing to you in your life is appearing because you are aligned to it. There is no right and wrong—there is only contrast. In contrast, you can align or be likened to something either by liking it or not liking it. This is the free will choice you have as a human. So if someone or something has shown itself to you in your life experience, you have drawn it to yourself in one of these two ways.

Why would you ever be angry, jealous, or upset or blame

someone or something for answering your call to all that is? You are a part of a reflective universe, and that reflection is your own.

Let Your Guidance System Serve You

Why do you feel good when we remind you there is love and you can choose it?

Don't you know that if this were a lie, you would know it?

You are incapable of not knowing the truth. Your guidance system is always telling you the truth, and all you need to do is listen to it. Ask it for the truth, and it will tell you.

The universe will never force you. You will always know by how you feel whether you are hearing the truth or not. If we told you that you're down here with no control over your life, that you might as well not even try, you'd know it wasn't true because it wouldn't feel good to you.

Trust the guidance system that responds with every thought you are choosing. Your guidance system is about you and the way you are thinking. It's not about whether the situation is in fact true or even going to happen. It's about the way you are thinking in respect to how your source is guiding you to think—that's what your guidance system is directing you upon.

Do you think this is happening randomly? How you feel as you read these words will tell you the truth. We know what the answer is because we know you and that you contain a truth meter.

When you feel good, your guidance system is telling you that the direction you are moving, the thoughts you are thinking, and the way you are feeling is headed in a direction that your experiences expanded you to and that you are going to be very happy with.

You may say things like, "I'm ruined. Nothing works for me. I have lost everything." The negative emotional charge is notification from your source that what you're thinking could cause a negative manifestation you do not want, so turn around. The human emotes from its experiences, but the source knows what it really wants and so sends the alert of a negative emotion to say, "Hey! Get back on track to what you really wanted."

Use this as a learning experience rather than a form of punishment. Your guidance system is serving you, helping you clean yourself up, so you can stay on the path that leads to what you want.

There is no belief, no idea, no suggestion, and no opinion that is worth what you are going to give up to enforce it. No one will ever align with you in your opposition to them. We're not saying you can't have a belief, an idea, or an opinion.

But you can never decide for another what theirs should be.

As the old saying goes, "You catch more flies with honey." There's no way you can be in alignment with someone as you argue with them. You are only going to invite what you are protesting against. If you are forcing what you believe onto another, you are inviting the energy of dominance to dominate, and all of your future interactions will be unpleasant.

To be whole, all of your emotions should be equal. When you allow yourself to be overwrought by anger, dominance, or control, you lose your balance. Now your other aspects of love, trust, and honor lose floor time. When any one emotion becomes too dominant, it stops the other emotions from being fully accessed and used in the life experience you are having. When you're out of balance, it's difficult to navigate your life experiences in understanding, which makes it harder for you to manifest what you want. Once your balance is thrown off, it's difficult to get that balance back.

Like we have said time and time again, every human has a right to sovereignty, an individual right to decide what they want to perceive and believe. As much as you want to think there is right and wrong, there is *not*. There are only perceptions based upon experiences. Sovereignty exists because each of you is a free creator.

You can set yourself free any time you decide to. Don't blame yourself, judge yourself, or dwell in experiences you have not enjoyed. Make a decision from here that you are a joy seeker, a lover of life, and a giver of freedom. What might the universe return to you based upon that perception?

Be quick to adjust yourself based upon the responses you receive from others. Know that pushing against anyone for any reason will continue to perpetuate conflict in your life.

"But they are wrong."

"They don't get it."

"They don't do the right things."

"They are not against what I think they should be against."

Why would you continue with a view that continues to notify you in negative emotion? Why would you not respond to yourself in how you feel? Why would you not value feeling *good* as much as you do as being *right*?

You have a guidance system that is for you, about you, and always with you.

Feel it. Use it, and let it be your guide.

CONCLUSION

WE ARE NOT HERE to hoodwink you. We are here to teach you that you can choose to have the life you want to have. We are here to, once and for all, show humans the gods they are and the power they hold.

In the midst of all of the chaos and contrast happening in the human world today, consciousness is rising. As more and more of you humans come into your power, you are realizing that you are creators. In your free will, you have the gift of choosing, picking, and deciding how you feel as you move through your lives.

Know One Thing: You Create

What does that mean?

There is nothing, no one, no situation, no way you are feeling—happy, sad, confused, jealous, joyous, loved, unloved, needy, satisfied, lonely, fulfilled, angry, irritated, confident, insecure—that you have not chosen as a result of how you perceived your life experiences. Everything you experience, *you* created.

What if, instead of becoming the experiences, you simply had them and did not attach to them? Remember you are a magnificent, loving, expansive, brilliant piece of what you call god who agreed to be an experiencer for all that is.

If you would remember this, you would materialize the reward you have earned by the experiences you contributed. You'd spend no time judging, condemning, and not loving yourself. You'd know how worthy you are as you are and how mistaken you were when you thought you had to do things perfectly. You came to feel, release, and grow—nothing more.

You are worthy as you are.

Self-Love Will Unlock the Door

We keep telling you you're not the tool, but you insist on becoming it and changing it into something you can deem as worthy. You fall back into old patterns of victimization. You have to recognize where your wound is, feel yourself falling back in an old pattern, and take responsibility for the experience you are experiencing.

Worthiness isn't something you must obtain by some false perception of perfection. Worthiness is a perception of love. Worthiness doesn't need to be a doctor. It doesn't need to be a lawyer. It doesn't need a big bank account. It doesn't need to look beautiful in other humans' eyes. It doesn't need to be admired by someone else. Worthiness is worthy of love. It's knowing that the moment you came to this plane and started having experiences, you became a worthy contributor to all that is. We don't care how small you think your contribution is. Everyone is contributing to expansion. Every single human, no matter how small or great they feel, is equal in creation in our eyes.

It's like watching a really good movie. You may be getting into it, but you never lose sight of the idea that it's not real—it's just something you're watching.

This is what happens to humans. This is a good movie you're in, and you can decide who the best actors are going to be. You are the lead actor in your own movie—and everyone else is the lead actor in theirs.

What if you were born on a remote island and never had any human contact. You would have no way to emote. You would have no one to love you, no one to argue with, no way to have an exchange so you could see how you were being received and how you were receiving them. You would have no way to grow. All of you experiencers are reflections of itself to itself, and those reflections draw to themselves like reflections so you may know yourselves as sovereign creators.

Self-love is the key that will unlock your door. It's not about being perfect. Self-love is achieved in the understanding that you are the source of love, and in the offering of love, it is mirrored back to you:

- How you can become an expression of source in your human form.
- How you choose to think and feel will be that expression.

Every one of you is a sovereign experiencer who has free will and gets to choose how they think and feel.

You Are Going to Change

You are going to change. You are going to be different. And you are going to finally make the shift.

Just the idea that you have condemned yourself is enough to ruin your plan.

The minute you decide there's something about yourself you don't like, the universe will say, "This one likes to judge themself," and the universe will support your view of yourself in the very condemnation it is receiving from you. You will continue in the same limiting patterns that have been holding you back, with mounting frustration that you are unable to transcend them. All the while, you are thinking you are not who you envisioned yourself to be, when in reality, you are exactly as you have envisioned yourself to be.

When you radiate feelings of disgust, distaste, and agitation, you become nothing more than a regenerator of it. You have to acknowledge that your human tool is having an emotion, but remember *you are not the human.* Let it blow right out the back door. Don't become the experience and condemn yourself for it. The universe isn't out to get you—it's out to understand what you want and bring it to you.

You're not going to get self-love through self-loathing. It will not work.

Change comes from the love, acceptance, and trust of self. The universe fulfills your desires because it matches you in your support of you.

Hold your desire for yourself in love, not in judgment. Every time you mess up, continue to love. In this way, your being will turn into that love. You only respond to what you offer. If you offer dissatisfaction of yourself, you will generate more things to be dissatisfied with. You can't get the you you want by hating the you you don't want.

Separation is a lack of understanding that affects your love of self. You humans love to justify your reasons you are not lovable. It's what you do when you become the tool. When you become the experience, your vibratory level dips, and it becomes harder and harder for your higher self to reach you. What you are feeling in your lowered state of emotive value is your source signaling you that you are moving in a direction that will not yield to you what you want. When you're connected to the source, you feel great. You feel as though you are governing your life and get a sense of satisfaction. Moving away from your higher self feels like all forms of negativity. The only reason you ever have a feeling of negativity is because the thoughts you are choosing are triggering a response from your source telling you that what you're perceiving in your present experience isn't in alignment to the experience that will bring you joy. The further you move away from the high vibratory level of yourself and all you have become from the life you have lived, the more despair you will feel.

Whatever you have a desire to experience, you are worthy to receive it. Don't follow a path because you think the path will make you worthy. Follow the path that makes you feel satisfied and fulfilled.

What makes your heart sing?

What are you happy doing?

Don't go after something outside of yourself because you think you're missing something inside of yourself. You are born with everything you need.

You are pure positive love experiencing contrast in the reality you are in. Stay connected in your love, and observe yourself in contrast.

Nothing is more important and more powerful than the perception you hold of yourself because this is the perception the universe will hold of you and what it will deliver on to you. Do you want the perception to be one that you hold? The one that you authentically are? Or do you want to live by the perceptions others hold of you? You are the only one who can decide.

Choose wisely.

ACKNOWLEDGMENTS

I WOULD LIKE TO THANK my husband, Dave, for his support and encouragement while writing this book—I could never have done it without him. His vision became my belief so that *Choose Your Universe* could arrive in form.

I am forever grateful to my editors Lisa and Anastasia, who worked tirelessly alongside Athena, Dave, and me, using their enormous skill and expertise to guide us on our journey. Another big thank you to Sophie, who assured our success by managing all of the important details that go into writing and publishing a book.

I want to thank my children, Brad and Mike, for all their loving support, which helped allow me to be all I was meant to be. Their input has helped more than they will ever know.

I would like to thank my daughter-in-law for allowing me to know what having a daughter feels like. To have a woman in my life who is supportive, kind, and understanding is a great blessing, and one my heart needed to experience. I'd like to express my gratitude to my sister, Heidi, who has been a continued support in the work we do together. Her knowledge and wisdom provided me with the courage to expand in ways I otherwise could not have. I have come to realize that "sister" means many things: friendship, guidance, understanding, a confidant, and a supporter of my growth and self-betterment.

Thank you to my special friends who have accepted me as I am and allowed me, without judgment, to fully express all of myself. You have loved and accepted this new part of me without forgetting the me I've always been, and I am forever grateful.

ABOUT THE AUTHOR

ROBIN JELINEK HAS SPENT MOST of her life researching the meaning of life and studying metaphysics. Continued practice led her to a Kundalini Awakening (a profound spiritual experience), which sparked incredible change within her and opened her body to receiving unfiltered information from the universe.

This book is a culmination of Robin's forty years of research, experience, and dedication. By sharing the information she receives, she hopes to help others who are seeking a new path in life or looking for an alternative source of information.

Robin is a wife, mother, and grandmother. She spends most of her time with her family, who have always been her priority and always will be.